HAIDAKHAN BABA

VIJAY GUPTA

HAIDAKHAN BABA

My years with the Himalayan Mystic

Translated by Namita Kala

HarperCollins *Publishers* India

First published in India by HarperCollins *Publishers* 2022
4th Floor, Tower A, Building No. 10, Phase II, DLF Cyber City,
Gurugram, Haryana – 122002
www.harpercollins.co.in

2 4 6 8 10 9 7 5 3 1

P-ISBN: 978-93-5629-274-1
E-ISBN: 978-93-5629-275-8

Typeset in 11.5/15 Adobe Garamond at
Manipal Technologies Limited, Manipal

Printed and bound at
Thomson Press (India) Ltd

MIX
Paper
FSC® C010615

This book is produced from independently certified FSC® paper
to ensure responsible forest management.

Dedicated to the lotus feet of Haidakhan Baba

CONTENTS

FOREWORD

Well-entrenched in Hinduism is the belief that God sometimes descends to earth as an avatar, that is, the manifestation of a deity that has assumed human form for some divine purpose. An avatar may also be defined as an incarnate divine teacher. Haidakhanwale Baba, or simply Baba Haidakhan, about whom this book has been written, qualifies as an avatar on both counts. He appeared out of a cave in 1970 near Haidakhan Village, seemingly out of nowhere, and proceeded to touch and transform the lives of millions of devotees who encountered Him. He taught us the eternal precepts of Truth, Simplicity and Love and emphasized the importance of Karma Yoga and Japa Yoga as protective shields in the troubled New Age we would be stepping into—the world in which we live today.

To trace the origins of Baba Haidakhan, one has to go back into pre-history to the time of his original incarnation as Mahavatar Baba, also described as Lord Sadashiv in the *Shiva Puranas*. He is said to have flashed through the millennia from time to time as a Guru Avatar, or in plainer words, an enlightened master, to instruct

His followers on the knowledge of the self and lead them to a higher plane of existence.

Unlike the more famous avatars of Lord Vishnu, such as Lord Ram and Lord Krishna, very little is known of Lord Shiva's avatars. Apart from Mahavatar Baba, Adi Shankaracharya and Dakshinamurti Bhagwan are also said to have been avatars of Lord Shiva. In fact, according to legend, the former, who gifted the world with Advaita Vedanta, received his initiation from Mahavatar Baba. Similarly, Lord Parashuram, the sixth avatar of Vishnu, is believed to have been sent to Him for penance after he had fulfilled his vow of vengeance to destroy all the kshatriyas in the world.

The prominent Shaivite revivalist, Lakulisha, credited with establishing the doctrine of the Pashupata and twelve jyotirlingas (Lord Shiva represented in phallic form) around India, is believed to have been an early manifestation of Babaji around 125 CE. Another manifestation of Babaji graced Tibet some six centuries ago as the well-known saint, Lama Baba.

In recent times, Lord Shiva has appeared on earth as Haidakhan Baba not once but twice. He appeared for the first time in the 1830s and trod the earth for a span of about ninety-odd years in this incarnation, enrapturing his followers with the many miracles He performed. He was last seen walking on the confluence of the rivers Kali-Gori in 1922 by a group of devotees, before turning into a ball of light and disappearing skywards. After a gap of nearly fifty years, He appeared once again in 1970 in the same village of Haidakhan which He had established in his previous incarnation, this time as a younger-looking eighteen-year-old boy. (It may be noted here that the old Haidakhan Baba was described as the Mahavatar Baba by both Paramhansa Yogananda and Lahiri Mahashaya).

The appearance of Lord Shiva as Haidakhan Baba was foretold in the famous Indian astrological treatise, the *Bhrigu Samhita*, written by the famous ancient astrologer saint, Maharishi Bhrigu. When

Babaji reappeared in His last incarnation, He spotted the young Vijay Gupta in Jaipur.

The author, Vijay Gupta, writes that he underwent his first mystical experience linked to Babaji at the Kathghariya Ashram as a thirteen-year-old before He reappeared. A few years later, after His *prakatya* (appearance), Babaji noticed the young Vijay, who was around sixteen at the time, and handpicked him as His personal buddy-cum-companion. Vijay went on to spend the remaining three years of his teenage life serving Babaji or, as he described it—'living in the company of God'.

Peppered with innumerable gripping, often funny, and always meaningful anecdotes, *Haidakhan Baba: My Years with the Himalayan Mystic*, is an eye-opener for the reader. It is a detailed and personal account of Vijay Gupta's spiritual journey, beginning with his boyhood spent with Lord Shiva in human form to his years as a young man, distracted by the world of politics, heedless of Babaji's warning that he would gain nothing by it; it records his subsequent disillusionment with the political firmament till he finally comes full circle back into the world which he had never really left. Tightly interwoven into the narrative is his unwavering, unshaken bond with Babaji, to which he remained true, even when he was at odds with Him.

A riveting account of God's various *leelas* in His latest incarnation, the book gives the reader a microscopic view of Vijay's life with Babaji, narrating to hilarious effect how he is often baffled by the inscrutable workings of His mysterious ways and divine purpose.

Haidakhan Baba is a tale of God in human form written by the chosen one. The book inevitably leads the reader to compare Vijay to Lord Ram's younger brother, Lakshman, or Lord Krishna's friend, Sudama.

Vijay's experiences are truly out of this world and are not likely to ever be repeated by any mortal soul who has been blessed with the company of God in human form. Vijay learns, first hand, the true meaning of love, truth and simplicity from his divine master. The book is a must-read for all spiritual seekers, as it serves as a guide to all those who are on a quest to understand what it is like to eat, live and sleep with Divinity.

(Honorary) Brigadier Dr Arvind Lal, Padma Shri,
Chairman, Haidakhandi Samaj

AUTHOR'S NOTE

Gurus have attracted accolades and reverence in all the religions of this world, because human prosperity and the redressal of evil and ill-fortune are only possible by the divine grace of a holy teacher. In our own era, Baba Haidakhan's descent to this world is worthy of veneration. His appearance itself is an impenetrable mystery, as no one really knows from where He came.

I have tried to faithfully recount the fourteen years that Babaji spent on this earth as accurately as memory permits, as providence provided me with the great good luck of following His divine footsteps and ascending several ladders of service in the period that I served Him.

Baba Haidakhan was a '*vitaraga*' karma yogi (a person who performs his duty without attachment) whose life reflected a natural transparency and simplicity. He empowered His devotees with diligence and was as much a servitor as they were, in every construction activity He undertook. Babaji did not administer discipline or sermonize from a lofty, remote pedestal. He worked shoulder to shoulder with them to help them achieve their dreams.

For the past two decades, Baba Haidakhan has been worshipped in Uttarakhand whilst simultaneously being recognized as a *Chiranjeevi.** Babaji stepped on to this earth to propagate dharma (virtue, duty), destroy adharma (evil), work for the greatest good and promote happiness during the course of His incarnation. He filled devotees with the joy of unwavering faith and endowed them with bliss through His myriad *leelas* (divine play, miracles).

In this book, I have striven to present the truth about Babaji as I saw it, knitting those rich experiences with all the beauty and feeling that I underwent at the time. Baba Haidakhan tried to provide His disciples with the right props to enable them to overcome the hardships of this world. It is with the hope that Babaji will continue to bless His followers with good fortune and grace them with His divine blessings that I write this book.

Vijay Gupta

---

* Literally, a 'long-lived soul', but used here in the spiritual context as the immortal one.

1

FOREVER GOD

Since time immemorial, Uttarakhand—land of gods or devbhoomi—tucked away in the verdant lap of the mighty Himalayas, has been home to sages seeking moksha or liberation from the cycle of birth and death. This sacred soil, where many great gurus have reincarnated, is also known as Kurmanchal.

I narrate here the story of the great guru, about whom tales have been handed down through the ages, retold as folklore, and documented even before His reincarnation as Guru Shri 1008 Haidakhanwale Baba.

Interestingly, several books had already been written about Babaji even before His reincarnation as Guru Shri 1008 Haidakhanwale Baba. These include *Mere Pyare Bhagwan Haidiyakandi* by Hemchand Joshi, *Shri Bhagwan Haidakhan Wale Baba* by retired Judge Late Girdhari Lal Misra, and the works of his younger brother, Late Acharya Vishnudutt Misra, a.k.a. Shastriji. The atman (soul) and essence of Baba Haidakhan still resides in His followers, and He remains loved and revered even today.

Following His reincarnation, Babaji's very first interaction with the local folk is very interesting. It took place in a village called

Haidakhan in district Nainital, Uttarakhand, in the foothills of Kurmanchal Kailash, where a stream of the river Gautami Ganga flows.

On its banks there is a natural cave, and it is here that Babaji first appeared in 1970, looking like an eighteen-year-old boy. Nothing is known of His parents. When questioned by the locals, Shri Haidakhan Babaji told them that He was the same Mahavatar Babaji*, the avatar of Lord Shiva, popularized amongst the people through the book, *Autobiography of a Yogi* by Shri Paramhansa Yogananda. He was the epitome of endless knowledge and divine powers during his life time (c. 1970 to 1984).

In his previous incarnation, the old Haidakhan Babaji is known to have appeared before different devotees at the same time; to some, as an old sage and to others, as a young mystic. There are even anecdotes that whenever two followers talked to Him together, both saw Him differently. This often led to arguments, as each saw Him in a different form and age. Babaji was omnipresent.

Although there is no information regarding His formal education, in his latest incarnation, we know He spoke several languages besides Hindi and Sanskrit. Devotees would speak to Him in Nepali, Gujarati, Urdu, English, and other languages, and He would respond in the same tongue. Another distinctive quality that set Him apart from ordinary people was the fragrance of *chandan* that emanated from his body. I can personally testify to this. He was reticent and spent most of His time in meditation.

The signs of His various incarnations are documented in the Shastras (ancient scriptures) and in twentieth-century records.** Shri

---

* Mahavatar means the Lord Himself in human form; not born of a mother's womb.

** Haidakhan Babaji's previous reincarnation is believed to have been the earlier, or 'old', Haidakhan Baba who appeared around c. 1800 in the Kumaon region and was seen to disappear in a ball of light in 1922.

Mahendra Maharajji (one of His foremost devotees) often talked about this. He had visitations from the old Haidakhan Baba and the Goddess Jagadamba in his childhood. Later on, the old Babaji appeared to him in a vision to greet him on his birthday and guided him through a session of intense meditation that lasted six days and six nights. Thereafter, the old Babaji disappeared.

Very eager to discover the location of Babaji's future incarnation, and wanting to find out everything that he could about Babaji, Mahendra Baba travelled extensively seeking the reincarnated Babaji. He journeyed across India, Nepal, Tibet, China, and later on mainly through the north and northwestern parts of India. After a long wait of twenty years, he was rewarded at last. Goddess Amba directed him in a dream to go to Kurmanchal where he would finally come face to face with Babaji.

Now that he was sure of Babaji's reincarnation, Mahendra Maharaj spread the word among the people, informing them that the great guru would soon appear for the betterment of the world. He worked day and night to restore Babaji's old temples and constructed some new ones, including those in Vrindavan and in Kathghariya near Haldwani. After Haidakhan Babaji appeared on the world's stage in 1970, these two shrines became famous as Kathghariya Dham Vishwashanti Tapovan and Samba Sada Shiva Kunj, respectively.

In *Autobiography of a Yogi*, Shri Paramhansa Yogananda speaks of Mahavatar Babaji as the 'deathless avatar'; Mahendra Maharaj also told his disciples that Haidakhan Babaji was the Lord Himself, an incarnation of Lord Shiva, and had not entered this world from a woman's womb. Shri Babaji assumed a series of such incarnations to guide followers about knowledge and dharma.

He too was considered a manifestation of Mahavatar Babaji. Mahendra Maharajji was his devotee, and after his disappearance, Babaji is said to have manifested before him many times.

There are many references to Haidakhan Babaji's previous incarnations in various books written between 1860 and 1922. Around 1860, He appeared out of a divine flame, and in 1922, He vanished as a ball of light in front of some people, while walking on the confluence of the Kali-Gori Ganga at the Nepal border. There are plenty of anecdotes that describe His divine powers, such as healing people, giving life to the dead, feeding a lot of people with very little food that never seemed to finish, changing forms, using water instead of ghee in yagnas, and giving darshan simultaneously to numerous people at different locations, etc.

Babaji had numerous visitors, and when He appeared in His next incarnation in 1970, there were still some followers who were familiar enough with His earlier avatar to make the connection between the two and recognize that He had returned.

2

KARMA YOGA AND THE POWER OF MANTRAS

Babaji reincarnated as Haidakhan Baba mainly to change malevolent hearts and once said, 'Meditation keeps your heart clean. How can God reside in an evil heart? A person who thinks of God incessantly always succeeds very easily in life. God is always there in his hour of need.' He stressed on the recitation of '*Om Namah Shivay*' along with other sacred chants. He stated that on doomsday, only these mantras would act as instruments of survival and only those truly devoted to God would survive. 'God,' he averred, is omnipotent.'

Although Babaji led a *Sanatan* (eternal) Hindu lifestyle and was revered accordingly, He was not a follower of any particular religion. Whenever he was asked which religion one should follow, His simple answer was 'follow whatever suits your heart', as 'every religion leads us to God'. Revered by people of all religious denominations, from all walks of life, and even by atheists, Babaji said that the world was one family, (*vasudhaiva kutumbakam*).

He encouraged followers to embrace truth, love and simplicity. These were the 'highest forms of any yoga,' He said, because they detached one from maleficent elements, including jealousy, anger, hatred, selfishness and violence. Babaji also emphasized karma yoga, i.e., selfless actions dedicated to God. Deeming it as the easiest path to Divinity, He introduced karma yoga as a mandatory part of the daily routine in the ashram at Haidakhan.

He stressed the importance of chanting mantras and following karma yoga. 'Being laborious in your actions is an innate quality of this path, and laziness is death. We should not run away from our duties. We should follow them. In today's world, inhumanity and idleness have increased among men. This is why it is very important not to surrender to such evils. We must believe in action.'

Babaji also talked about mutual respect to His devotees (many of them from Europe and the United States) through books, interviews, and even in their dreams. He never craved fame.

In the first two years of His incarnation, Haidakhan Baba spoke very little, but in the ensuing twelve years He conversed very easily. He gave discourses but stressed more on chanting mantras during religious congregations. The sound of '*Om Namah Shivay*' always reverberated at our gatherings. It is still incessantly recited at our ashram today because it leads to the tryst between the atman and God.

A follower once asked Him why He did not deliver sermons very often. He smiled and replied, 'I am enabling you in a way that will ensure that whenever I address you, you become totally absorbed, unlike the indiscriminate discourses given by various sages who fail to captivate their audience.'

Babaji said that at the end of Kalyuga, i.e., Kali yuga, the age of darkness, mankind would be in extreme danger, and there would be a marked lack of spirituality in the world. He prophesied that it was only then that people would chant the eternal truth in the name of God and understand the meaning of 'Brahman'. A new world would evolve through them.

3

THE FIRST VISITATION

Writing about Babaji and His divine powers is a herculean task, because He evokes feelings that cannot be articulated through mere words. I restrained myself from writing about my experiences in the past, because Babaji is Lord Shiva Himself. To write about something that is so esoteric in nature, a journey that is so spiritual in thought and deed, cannot be written without His celestial guidance.

After Haidakhan Babaji took samadhi in 1984, I would often cry for hours on end as I did not have His deific company anymore. But then I would rise again, feeling blessed because I had had the honour of accompanying Him everywhere for about fourteen years after He appeared in 1970 to play out his divine mission.

Nevertheless, in the years following 1984, in fact for years afterwards, I couldn't write a word, even after receiving tons of constant requests from Haidakhan Babaji's followers, both in India and abroad; such was the irony. I would read books by other writers on Him and feel the urge to write. So after thirty-six long years, I have decided to pen a book under His divine guidance and place my experiences before my readers to guide them and take them on the spiritual journey I once embarked upon as a young teenager.

Members of my family were devotees of Mahendra Maharaj, prime among them being my elder brother, Shivcharan Lal. I was lucky enough to enjoy several blissful interactions with Swamiji. However, before I write about this divine reincarnation of Lord Shiva Himself, it is my duty to tell you about Mahendra Maharajji, because it was thanks to his incessant meditation that Babaji reincarnated as Bhagwan Haidakhan.

A paragon of peace and dedication, Mahendra Baba considered himself an insignificant devotee of the great Atman. Mahendra Maharajji's followers regarded him as an incarnation of Goddess Amba. People felt blessed in his company, and their wishes were granted. Swamiji constructed a temple dedicated to Babaji in Vrindavan, which drew large multitudes, and to our great surprise, he made Vishnudutt Misra (Shastriji) write several books on Babaji's future incarnation even before He reincarnated.

Swamiji also constructed a room next to Babaji's idol in Vrindavan and made daily offerings inside it. He told us that Babaji would stay there when He arrived. Swamiji undertook rigorous *tapasya* (penance) to pray for Babaji's reincarnation, especially meditating at Shitla Khet near Almora in Uttarakhand. His followers from Uttar Pradesh, Rajasthan, Gujarat, Maharashtra, Bihar and Madhya Pradesh would often come to Vrindavan to visit him, and I too was blessed with his presence quite often.

I was around thirteen or fourteen years old at that time and had grown up in a religious environment. One bhajan (devotional song) stands out distinctively from my childhood: '*Mujhe apna bana loge to kya hoga, sharan dekar, meri bigdi bana doge to kya hoga?*' (What will happen if you make me yours, what will happen if you restore what I have spoilt?); I would often hum it.

Babaji's first idol was established in Vrindavan. My family assembled for the inauguration of the second one in Kathghariya

Ashram, located seven kilometres from Haldwani in Uttarakhand. The idol was installed with all due rituals in the presence of a number of devotees and sadhus who had gathered there along with Mahendra Maharajji.

It was a moment of perfect happiness in my life.

Situated beside a canal, Kathghariya Ashram was a beautiful place surrounded by mountains. The ashram had a school adjacent to it. The followers who had congregated for the inauguration were staying nearby.

On the day the idol was installed, the whole ashram resounded with chants of '*Om Namah Shivay*' and bhajans like '*O Haidakhan wale humko na bhul jana, jeevan nisha mai tum chand banke aana*' (O Haidakhan Baba don't ever forget us, come as the moon into the darkness of our life). I watched the whole scene with wide-eyed curiosity. At around 9 p.m. that evening, a devotee came shouting, 'Look! The kurta-topi Baba is here!' and a stampede broke out. Someone said, 'I can see Him on the face of the moon!'

Mahendra Maharajji smiled, amused by the excitement and curiosity of his followers. Just then, a devotee said, 'Look at that jyoti, Babaji is inside it!' All of us stood in a row and watched, enraptured, as a small flame floated before us; sometimes up, sometimes down, sometimes on the mountains, sometimes on a bell. This went on for about an hour. It was our first encounter with Babaji's divine *leela*, and it was a magical experience for everyone present. A sense of benediction pervaded the air. Swamiji continued to smile quietly as he watched the divine play, unfold. Soon after, the priest offered food to the idol. A few minutes later, he was astonished to find that part of it had been eaten; 'Prabhu (the deity) has had His share of the prasad,' Mahendra Maharajji remarked.

Kirtans were sung throughout that night. In the morning, the priest came and informed everyone that Babaji had slept in the room that Swamiji had built next to the idol, as there were tiny footprints on His bed. When devotees clamoured for an answer, Mahendra Maharajji smiled and replied, 'It is all Prabhu's *leela*.' Several devotees trooped into the room to take photographs of those footprints, which were later printed in a book.

The devotional gathering went on for three days, and even after returning home to Bharatpur, my native place in Rajasthan, I couldn't forget those magical moments. I still remember the divine flame and feel eternally blessed by those visions that took place before His reincarnation.

4

SWAMIJI DEPARTS

The wheel of time continued apace, until one day Mahendra Maharajji called his followers to Vrindavan. 'The body is mortal,' he told his devotees, 'and life can leave anyone, anytime; everyone has to go one day.' He then disclosed the all-important question that was worrying him—'How are you all going to recognize Babaji when He comes to earth in His next Avatar? It is my strong belief that He will definitely be reincarnated.'

The followers were perplexed, and Acharya Vishnudutt Shastri, keen to find a solution, asked Swamiji to guide them.

'Dear brother Vishnu,' Swamiji replied, with a smile, 'I am going to reveal a mantra to you, which is known to no one but Haidakhan Babaji and me. Anyone who comes to you and claims that he is Babaji, must chant this mantra without being asked for it. If you hear this mantra from someone without asking for it, you will know that He is the reincarnation of Haidakhan Baba'—and later gave the mantra to Shastriji. Then he told us what Lord Krishna had told Arjuna in the Mahabharata: 'the wheel of time never stops; one should spare time and comply with one's duty; this is *manav dharma*, (the guiding principle for man).'

In June 1969, Mahendra Maharaj left his body. He was cremated on the banks of the Yamuna at Vrindavan. The great saint had left us with the words 'Baba *jaroor ayenge*' (Baba will definitely come), and we, his devotees, held on to that belief and kept waiting for the prophecy to be fulfilled.

5

BABAJI ARRIVES

As the winter of 1970 approached, Mahendra Maharajji appeared in the dreams of many devotees and spread the word of Babaji's reincarnation. Several of them started visiting Haidakhan. And in October 1970, Baba Haidakhan appeared for the first time in a cave on the far side of Adi Kailash. This is where He was found by a villager of Haidakhan.

The nearest town to Haidakhan is Haldwani and the nearest station, Kathgodam. Today, vehicular traffic is a common sight at the ashram, but in those days, devotees had to trudge from Kathgodam across the mountain on foot to reach Haidakhan Ashram, as there were no approach roads. The story of how the Haidakhan Village got its name is also fascinating. There are many *Harra* trees (*Terminalia chebula*) and '*khande*' or boulders in the area. The two words were combined together to coin the single word Haidakhande, and so the village got its name.

Haidakhan Ashram is a beautiful place with the Adi Kailash (a mountain peak named after the original Kailash in Tibet) towering on one side. The mountain is famous among locals as the place where Lord Shiva's wedding procession rested on His return from

His marriage to Ma Sati. There is a sati kund (sacred pond) in the foothills of the Adi Kailash where Ma Sati is said to have bathed, according to local lore. A huge ancient tree fringes the kund and bears silent witness to that bygone age.

There is also an ancient Shiva temple in Haidakhan. Even the elders who live there locally are unable to say how old it is. The Shivling in this temple is similar to the one in Kedareshwar, and it is my personal experience that people who pray in this temple with utmost devotion are granted every wish they make to the Lord.

6

BABAJI CATCHES ME

My elder brother worked in the railways and was stationed in Agra. One day, he came home to Bharatpur and announced that we would all be proceeding to Haidakhan on the Kathgodam Express—the only train which ran between Agra and Kathgodam—for Babaji's darshan. I tried to pull all kinds of excuses to get out of the trip, as I was told that we would have to walk 22 kilometres from Kathgodam to reach the ashram, a long distance to cover on foot. The train was to depart from Agra Fort at 8 p.m. Everyone was packing, while I kept searching for a pretext to weasel out of the journey.

The next day, we started out from Bharatpur to Agra to catch the train and reached the city at around six in the evening. As the time of departure drew closer, I was still looking for an exit option. At 7:30 p.m. I told Shivcharan bhaisahib, my elder brother, that I had a severe stomach ache. He asked me to take some medicine for it, while the rest of the family assured me that I would be fine. I accepted the medication that was proferred to me with good grace and swallowed it manfully. The stomach ache would have definitely disappeared if I'd had one to begin with. But, having decided that I was not going to Haidakhan come what may, I told everyone that the ache had worsened and they should carry on without me, as I did not want to impede their enjoyment of the trip.

The train was ready to leave. My brother once again asked whether my tummy felt better. I shook my head firmly and said, 'No.'

The train moved, and I stood on the platform trying my best to look forlorn. My martyred air must have been quite convincing, as my gambit paid off. I went back to my cousin's place in Agra. He naturally asked me why I had stayed back, and I plied him with the sob story that I had told the others. Two days later, I returned to Bharatpur, beginning to feel the stirrings of regret for not making it to the ashram.

The rest of the family came back a week later and inundated me with stories about Haidakhan. They told me that Babaji was the living form of Lord Shiva Himself and would be soon coming to Vrindavan. All the trustees of the Vrindavan temple had apparently landed up at the Haidakhan Ashram and requested Babaji to pay a visit. He had agreed.

Later, when we were alone, my elder brother divulged that during their visit to Haidakhan, Babaji had been in the cave. He was wearing a loin cloth, and His body was covered in ash. Then came the embarrassing part. 'When I told Him that you could not make it because you were unwell, He said, "Your younger brother was just conning you. There is nothing wrong with him".'

He speared me with a stern look and asked me if it was true. I told him the truth and confessed that I had been pulling a fast one. I felt extremely mortified. I was also surprised that Babaji had known what I was up to, even though He was so many miles away. From then on, I was filled with a strange craving to see Babaji and could not wait to meet Him. His visit to Vrindavan was just a few days away.

My period of waiting was over. The moment arrived, and my elder brother informed us that Babaji would be reaching Vrindavan the following day. He told me that now was the time for me to go and get His darshan. The next morning, I took the train to Vrindavan via Mathura. I just had to see Babaji!

7

BABAJI AT FIRST SIGHT

The temple in Vrindavan is located alongside Gopinath Bazaar, near the Brahmkund. It was quite crowded. As soon as I entered, I saw a young sadhu seated on a wooden bed-like bench called a 'takht'. The hall was lined with long queues of devotees waiting for darshan. I joined them, inching my way closer to Babaji, impatiently awaiting my turn. I was quickly falling under His spell. His face emanated a powerful radiance and His dreadlocks were golden; there was a *tripund*—three horizontal lines drawn with *chandan* (sandalwood paste)—on His forehead, and He was sitting in a meditative state clad in a kurta, His legs covered by an *andi*, a sheet, that hung from His shoulders. After the darshan, I sat in a corner and watched Him closely. I could not take my eyes off Him. The urge to go on looking at Him was too strong.

The whole temple was echoing with chants of '*Haidakhandi, Haidakhandi Bol*'. A kirtan was being sung, and I became so absorbed in the spiritual ambience of the place that I forgot to go back home. I was surrounded by some natives of the Haidakhan village who had accompanied Babaji to Vrindavan. One of them, Chandramani, was telling devotees about His reincarnation. I listened very carefully.

He told us that Babaji had reincarnated in a natural cave beside the holy Gautami Ganga River after forty-plus years since the end of His previous incarnation. This was His fifth incarnation. Chandramani said his late father had served Him in His previous Avatar.

He told us that Babaji had appeared to him in a dream and asked him to come to the cave situated at the bottom of Adi Kailash to serve him. Chandramani had awoken with a start. Unable to go back to sleep, he had roused his son and wife and told them that Babaji had come back. He was in a cave and was calling him. Determined to go to Him that very night, Chandramani asked his wife to prepare a *thali* of fruits and milk. He then crossed the river in the dark, traversing at least a kilometre to reach Him.

And there he found Him—a slim, fair, sharp-featured handsome young sadhu, lost to the world, immersed in meditation, clad in a loincloth with an *andi* hanging from His shoulder and covering His torso and legs. Chandramani bowed to Him and sat in a corner, patiently waiting for Him to return to consciousness.

After some time, the young sadhu opened His eyes. Chandramani bowed, addressing Him as Lord Haidakhan. He recounted his dream and asked the sadhu, 'How can I serve you? What are your orders for me?'

Babaji smiled. He raised His hand and blessed him.

Soon afterwards, Babaji went up to Adi Kailash and devoted Himself to rigorous penance for forty-five days, accepting nothing but water and sometimes milk from Chandramani who went there each day to serve Him.

8

A MIRACLE ON THE MOUNTAIN TOP

Chandramani told us how he would climb up to Adi Kailash each day from the village. The nearest water source, the Gautami Ganga, was 4 kilometres away. Babaji had instructed Chandramani to bring up a canister of water every day. It must be mentioned here that there was nothing edible to be found in the vicinity. A wooden plank stood beside a short wall nearby. It was full of bells tied by people who visited the place every Monday.

Babaji meditated on Adi Kailash for forty-five days. Each day, Chandramani trekked up via the Gautami Ganga with a full canister of water, and on rare occasions offered Him some milk too, which Baba sometimes accepted, but only after much urging. He firmly refused any solids.

One day, said Chandramani, a miracle occurred. As he approached Babaji's meditation spot he stumbled and the canister he had been carrying on his shoulders slipped. All the water fell out. He quietly went and sat down. After some time, when Babaji came out of His meditative state, He asked Chandramani why he was so downcast.

Chandramani told Him what had happened and asked for permission to go back and fetch more water. Babaji smiled and said, 'Look, bhakt (devotee), what's in that mountain?' Chandramani looked and saw that the mountains were glittering with gold. He felt a sense of utter bliss and exclaimed, 'Lord, that mountain is golden.' Babaji smiled again and told him, 'Look at the canister of water you have been talking about.' Chandramani could not believe his eyes. The canister stood erect and was full of water.

There were many such anecdotes from His previous avatar as well, handed down to Chandramani by his father. He proceeded to narrate them to us.

9

CHANDRAMANI HAS MORE TALES TO TELL

One fine morning, the chief gardener of the VIP guest house (referred to as the governor's house later), in the vicinity of the temple, a devotee of Baba (in his previous incarnation) was preparing tea in a small brass pot (called a lota). Babaji dropped in for a visit along with ten followers. The gardener panicked, but Babaji told him not to worry. 'Just pour the tea you made for yourself from that lota.' The brass pot was too small to contain enough tea for so many people. Nevertheless, the gardener did as he was told.

To his great surprise, the tea did not run out, and after he had served everyone, there was still some left over. After a while, some 200 devotees showed up for Babaji's darshan, and again, Babaji instructed the gardener to serve them all tea from the same lota. Once again, to his acute astonishment, the tea proved sufficient. Even after serving all 200 of them, there was still some left over! Over time, His miracles became a byword.

He told us another story from Babaji's previous incarnation. Pandit Haridutt Pant was posted at the Commissionerate. The British Raj was at its zenith, and in winters, the Commissionerate would shift to Haldwani from Nainital. Hariduttji was going to Haridwar from Haldwani for a holy dip in the Ganges during the Kumbh. He had sent his luggage ahead to the railway station. An hour before the train departed, he headed to the station with his friends. On the way, a gentleman told him that Babaji was in town. He asked the gentleman for His direction, which was duly provided.

Pandit Haridutt Pant met Babaji at the address and prostrated on the ground at His feet. Lord Haidakhan asked him where he was off to, and Pantji apprised Him of his itinerary.

Babaji said, 'Okay go. Make sure you bathe in the Ganges. We are also thinking of going there for a snan (bath). We might meet you there.'

Pandit Haridutt took his leave and reached the station, where he kept a look out for Babaji but couldn't spot Him. Disappointed, he sat in the train and reached Haridwar the next morning. When he went to *Har Ki Pauri* to take a dip with his friends, a surprise awaited him. He espied Babaji bathing on the same ghat. When he found out that there was no other train to Haridwar, he surmised that Babaji had flown in!

There was an even greater surprise in store for Pandit Haridutt when he returned to Haldwani. People told him that they had seen Babaji bathing near Chitrashila in Ranibagh that morning. Locals used to swear that He could fly, and some of them even admitted to having spotted Him in the act. He would also appear to His devotees in different places at the same time.

It was such pleasure to hear Chandramani's stories about Babaji. I felt deeply envious. He was so very lucky to have had the honour to serve Him and witness the divine play that established that Babaji was Lord Shiva incarnate.

10

SOME PRIESTS PROTEST

When devotees found out about Haidakhan Babaji's scheduled arrival at Vrindavan, they organized a procession and seated Him on an elephant. On reaching the temple, they took Him to the room that had been constructed for Him by Mahendra Maharaj some twenty odd years ago; a room adjacent to the idol of Lord Haidakhan. Offerings of Tulsi (holy basil) leaves and flowers were being made to Babaji when raised voices were heard outside the temple. Some local priests from other temples in Vrindavan were protesting. They thought that such offerings should only be made to Lord Krishna and not to any mortal or Baba.

An altercation broke out between Babaji's devotees and the protesting priests. The former had a point. They told the priests that they revered Babaji the same way the latter worshipped Lord Krishna and said, 'You can't question our faith.'

As tempers rose to a boil and a clash looked imminent, the trustees of the temple went to Babaji, who asked, 'What is going on, who is making such a loud racket?'

Laxminarayanji, the president of the trust, explained the situation to Babaji, who heard him out patiently and told him to bring the local priests in. Once they arrived, He told them gravely, 'Don't think this saint is a toy. If you make the mistake of clashing with us, the outcome will not be good for you.'

Immediately after uttering these words, He rose and went to His room.

Babaji's words caused a stir among the local priests. They exchanged mute glances and suddenly changed their stance. They abandoned their earlier aggression and left without any further ado.

I could not understand how one word from Him had had such a major impact on them. He was definitely a saint to be reckoned with.

11

SWAMIJI'S FATHER PUTS BABAJI TO TEST

There were whispers in the temple that a devotee had been dispatched to Rajgarh to fetch Vishnudutt Shastri. I had been in Vrindavan for the past two days and didn't feel like going back home. I was really enjoying the atmosphere around me, meeting other devotees, listening to kirtans, receiving Babaji's darshan—I was in bliss. I would go to the temple at around five in the morning. Babaji would come out of His room at around 9 a.m. and a long queue of devotees would be waiting to see Him.

At around ten that morning, an old man's visit took everyone by surprise. Disciples of the late Mahendra Baba ran to welcome him. The old man was Swamiji's father. He was received with utmost respect and seated on an *aasan* (a large cushion used for sitting). He asked Shri Laxminarayanji and Chetramji whether the sadhu at the temple was Haidakhan Baba. They answered in the affirmative. A fragrance of flowers and incense sticks pervaded the temple. Chants of '*Om Namah Shivay*' permeated the air as devotees patiently waited for Babaji to come out of His meditative state. They would turn ecstatic whenever His unique eyes rested on them and would feel as though all their desires had been fulfilled.

Something was preying on the old man's mind. All of a sudden, he took out some black grams and threw them at Babaji. This outraged some devotees, but they kept silent as he was Swamiji's father. One of them, however, dared to make a satirical comment. 'What are you doing? What do you think you'll achieve? There is a saying that tantrics are very irate by nature.'

Swamiji's father hailed from Darbhanga in Bihar, a state in eastern India. Tantra is an integral part of the lives of people from Bihar and neighbouring states like Bengal and Assam.

Responding to the intrepid devotee, Mahendra Maharaj's father said, 'If you want to see the power of a single gram, then keep quiet and watch. If I throw one gram empowered by mantras on the road, that jeep coming from Pagal Baba's temple won't be able to cross this temple.' And to demonstrate his point, he recited some mantras and threw a single gram in the general direction of the jeep. To our immense astonishment, the jeep screeched to a halt and couldn't cross the temple. It had developed some mechanical fault and broken down!

There was a terrified silence. Swamiji's father smiled and said, 'If one gram has so much power, you can imagine the effect of the amount I threw at the sadhu. Had He been a conman, the takht would have been over Him, and He would have been under it. The Person who has taken over my son's seat is a major sage. He is a great saint, and it is difficult to say anything else about Him.'

Just then, Babaji's eyes flew open. The old man approached Babaji for His blessings and left the ashram with all due respect.

12

MAHENDRA BABA MEETS HIS FATHER

Pandit Ramgopal Sharma, a postmaster, devotee, and one of the trustees of the Vrindavan temple, told us about Shri Mahendra Maharaj's father. The story goes like this: Shri Mahendra Maharaj wanted to visit his native place in the year that he left his body. He asked Pandit Ramgopal Sharma to accompany him, and they set out for Darbhanga by car. Once they reached his home, he bowed before the house, picked up some soil and rubbed it on his brow. Only then did he call out for someone to open the door.

A young fellow appeared and asked who they wished to meet. Swamiji asked for his father, referring to him by his given name. The young fellow informed them that the old gentleman was not at home but added, 'He'll be back soon.'

The lad then asked Swamiji for his name, to which Swamiji replied, 'I'll disclose my name to the gentleman I wish to meet, when he arrives.' Bowing before his house once again, Swamiji paid obeisance to the soil of his native place and returned to the car. He asked Sharmaji to start the car and drive back. Shri Mahendra

Maharajji was peaceful by nature. People knew him as Brahmchari Baba (a sage who has taken the vow of celibacy).

Continuing with the tale, Sharmaji told us, 'We had travelled about 40 kilometres when I thought, Mahendra Baba came home and did not even meet his father. I wondered why. Even though I was curious, I found myself unable to say anything. Finally, I could not help myself and mustered up the courage to ask, "Prabhu, you came home and did not even meet your father. Why?" But Mahendra Maharaj just smiled.'

Sharmaji reminisced, 'The Ambassador car was moving. I was lost in thought when suddenly, after two hours of driving, the car stopped at Swamiji's house!'

Pandit Ramgopal Sharma was astounded. How had this happened? Mahendra Baba got out of the car, and Sharmaji followed suit. An old man came to them and Swamiji touched his feet. Sharmaji followed suit. The old gentleman invited them inside and offered them refreshments. Only then did he ask, 'How are you Mahendra?' and demanded to know why Swamiji had not told the young lad his name and why had he left without meeting him.

Swamiji's father then described how he had managed to get the visitors back to his door. 'I used my tantric powers and said let those who were here come back.' Sharmaji told us he felt blessed in the older man's presence, and his curiosity evaporated.

This then is the background of Swamiji's father and should help readers understand what a great tantric he was. I was impressed that even a tantric like him had touched Babaji's feet. It just went to prove that Babaji was God indeed.

13

BABAJI PASSES ANOTHER TEST

My family had also arrived at Vrindavan to meet Babaji, and my elder brother, who liked singing bhajans, regaled several to the accompaniment of a harmonium. Acharya Vishnudutt Shastriji came from Rajgarh the next day, and all eyes were on him; what would he tell us about Babaji?

Babaji was in deep meditation, and Shastriji went and sat in a corner after bowing before Him. Babaji used to meditate several hours a day at the time.

That day, He opened His eyes at around 11 a.m. and called Ramesh Sharma—a devotee from Lohvan—and whispered something in his ears. Ramesh went to Shastriji and passed on the message. Shastriji rose and followed Ramesh. As as they drew close to Him, Babaji quickly got up and went into the room that Mahendra Baba had built adjacent to the idol.

Shastriji followed Him in. Babaji sat on His *aasan* and told Shastriji to shut the door. He complied and they were in the room for quite a while. Just as we were beginning to wonder how long they would take, Shastriji came out and announced:

'As the Acharya of the Haidakhandi Society, I hereby declare that this sadhu is the true reincarnation of Shiva and the Haidakhanwale Baba. We should have no doubts about this. You are aware that before leaving his body Mahendra Baba had called us all to Vrindavan and asked us how we would recognize Babaji when He arrived, since he would not be there to identify Him. For this purpose, he disclosed a mantra to me secretly and told me that it was the key to recognizing the true reincarnation.

'He said if one day someone comes to this temple and claims He is Haidakhan Baba, He will recite the mantra to you thrice, without being asked for it. And you mustn't have any doubts about the sadhu after that, because He will be the true Haidakhan Baba. Today, Babaji recited the mantra to me thrice of His own accord and asked me if I still had any doubts. I told Him that He had removed them all.'

Shastriji's words dispelled all the remaining reservations that had lingered among devotees about Babaji being the reincarnated Lord Haidakhan. Everyone was happy and relieved.

My brother gave me permission to return home, but by this time I was reluctant to leave. I told him that I would go back to Bharatpur after two days. Later that evening, I found out that Babaji would be leaving for Gwalior in five days.

14

BABAJI AND THE RECALCITRANT PRIEST

The next day a strange thing happened. There was a theft in the temple. Babaji had been at Vrindavan for barely six days. A devotee from Mumbai had gifted a gold pendant weighing thirty grams to the temple, to be placed on Babaji's idol, and it had gone missing. Even after much search and inquiry, no clues turned up.

Suspicion soon fell on the temple priest, who had been appointed by the late Mahendra Maharaj several years ago. The priest had been well looked after in the twenty years that he had served the temple. He had been given a house adjacent to the temple to ease his burdens. His son Gopal's education and wedding had both been funded at the temple's expense, and if this were not enough, a dharamshala (rest house for pilgrims) had been constructed and named Gopal Bhavan, after the said offspring, to provide the priest with an additional income.

When the pendant disappeared, the priest claimed that he knew nothing about it, but nobody believed him. Whispers grew, and word of the incident reached Babaji's ears. He called Laxminarayanji—president of the Vrindavan temple trust—and asked him what had happened. Laxminarayanji nervously brought Babaji up to date with all that had taken place. Babaji told him to call the priest.

The priest was sitting outside the temple door when Laxminarayanji went to him. The priest immediately got on his high horse and refused to heed the summons. 'Tell Babaji that I cannot come right now.' Laxminarayanji was torn. On the one hand, he was bound by Babaji's orders, and on the other hand, he was facing the priest who had been chosen by Mahendra Maharajji. He didn't know what to do. Just then a devotee arrived and told him, 'Babaji is calling you.'

He went in, in a dismal frame of mind, and told Babaji what the priest had said. He was told to go back and repeat the summons. Laxminarayanji returned to the priest and repeated Babaji's message.

Intransigent, the priest said angrily, 'I have already said I will not come.'

Laxminarayanji returned and relayed the priest's words. Babaji was furious. His eyes turned red. He folded his hands into a fist, twisted it thrice and said, 'Priest, come here.'

Almost immediately, the priest appeared before Babaji, huffing and puffing because he had sprinted all the way. 'Yes, Prabhu,' he said.

Babaji questioned him about the pendant. The priest denied all knowledge of it. Babaji repeated the question. Once again, the priest claimed ignorance. Babaji finally said, 'Listen, you must leave the premises before the sun sets.'

He told Laxminarayanji to let the priest take whatever valuables he wanted from the temple. 'Do not stop him, as he has worshipped the idol of Haidakhan Baba.' He vowed in the name of Goddess Laxmi that He would not drink water until the priest left the premises. With these words, He shut the door of His room and bolted it.

The priest took Babaji at His word. He not only loaded his own belongings, but also a number of valuables that belonged to the temple in three tempos and forsook Vrindavan for the rest of his life.

The entire operation took place in a space of three hours, and we all stood by silently and watched him leave. I later learnt that he had gone back to his village, Lohvan, which was just 8 kilometres away.

At around five in the evening, Laxminarayanji and some other devotees went to Babaji with some *bhog* (food offered to deities) and water. Babaji opened the door and asked Laxminarayan, 'Did you try to stop him from taking anything?'

Laxminarayanji said, 'No Prabhu, he took whatever he wanted.'

Babaji smiled. 'Why are you so anxious? Everything will be alright now.'

After the priest left, I overheard Laxminarayanji saying, 'It's so hard to kick out a bad tenant these days, even if they've only been in occupation for just two years. Yet Babaji managed to get rid of this priest, who was here for twenty years, in just four hours.'

15

BABAJI AT BHARATPUR

I came back to Bharatpur. My brother told me that Babaji would be coming for a three-day stay before going on to Bandikui. His itinerary was: from the mountains to Vrindavan, then on to Gwalior, Bharatpur and Bandikui. Babaji had been in Gwalior at Laxminarayanji's place for the past seven days. Everyone started preparing for His arrival. Rations were stored and arrangements made for His stay and for the accommodation of His devotees. The list of to-do items was endless.

A big bus with lights and a special rooftop *aasan* had been arranged for His entry into town. My brother wanted a procession to escort Babaji to our house. A band was at the ready, along with a group of kirtan singers. My brother left for Gwalior to pick up Babaji, even as our house was being decorated like a bride for Him.

Babaji reached Bharatpur by the evening train. My family, some close friends, and devotees from near and far, all gathered at the platform to receive Him with flowers and garlands.

The train inched into the platform and jubilations broke out. My brother waved from the first-class compartment, signalling us to come forward in an orderly fashion. With the kind of enthusiasm that had been building up, it was hardly surprising when a stampede broke out, and everyone surged forward to welcome Lord Haidakhan.

As He got off the train, He was swamped by the milling crowd. What small feet He had! And they were bare. We went to Him one by one and literally inundated Him with garlands. The entire station echoed with voices yelling, '*Bhole Baba ki Jai*'. Passers-by stopped in their tracks to gaze at His magnetic face.

Someone exclaimed, 'Look! How beautiful He is! He looks like a young boy!'

A bus was standing outside the station for Babaji's devotees. We escorted Babaji and a few of His close companions to a car. Outside our house there was another bus—the one with the special rooftop *aasan* and the lights. It was about 7:30 p.m. by now, and the top of the bus had been lit up. Two bands in front of it were playing spiritual tunes. *Jaikara* (acclamations and cheers) were being raised on the mic. Babaji went into our house briefly and then came out. Perhaps He had wanted to quench His thirst. We later found out that He did not even drink water in front of anyone.

He seemed very young and innocent and readily agreed to do whatever His devotees requested. On this occasion, He was asked to grace the procession which was to go through all the main routes of the city and culminate at our house.

Babaji was helped up to the top of the bus via a ladder at its rear end. Some devotees also sat on the roof with Him. The band struck a new note and marched forward. The bus inched ahead slowly, accompanied by a cavalcade of devotees. Sounds of '*Bhole Baba ki Jai*' resounded. A few followers sang bhajans as they walked with the bus. The procession went through all the main roads and finally returned to our house. We were home at last!

Babaji climbed down from the bus, and we took Him to the room we had prepared for Him. There was a dharamshala nearby where food and lodging had been arranged for all the devotees. It was around 9 p.m. by now. My brother went to Babaji with some prasad only to discover that He did not eat grain. His diet consisted of milk at night, curd or butter milk in the morning and a couple of slices of any fruit or orange juice in the afternoon. He would neither eat, nor drink water, in front of everyone. Food had to be placed in His mouth lovingly. This is what my brother told us.

His daily itinerary was equally fascinating. He would go to bed at 10 p.m. and wake up at 4 a.m. There was a proper bathing process for Babaji, which involved filling buckets separately with water, milk and curd. They were then mixed with Ganga jal (holy water from the Ganges). At five in the morning, He would apply *chandan* on his forehead and then on the brows of all His devotees. By 10 p.m. He would retire to His room and shut the door.

My brother began to make preparations for His bath the previous night itself. It was as if his sleep had vanished! He cleaned the bathroom and filled four or five buckets with water. Milk was poured into one bucket early the next morning. Curd was put into another pail, and Ganga jal was mixed into the water. By 3 a.m., my brother was ready for Babaji's morning ablutions. The rest of the family was also on stand-by. We were to discover shortly that during His bath, Babaji would sit on a chowki (a short wooden platform with legs) and devotees would pour water over Him and take care of the nitty-gritty of His bath, just as they would for any idol of Lord Shiva.

Babaji's door opened at 4 a.m. Some devotees went with my brother into His room. Babaji came out in a kurta and headed straight for His bath.

'Doesn't He go to the toilet?' I asked. A devotee satisfied my curiosity and told me that He did not, because He was the Lord Himself. No one had ever seen Him going to the washroom.

Babaji sat on the chowki after devotees had helped Him out of His kurta, and they began pouring water over His body. Some poured it over His torso, others at His feet. Then milk and curd were massaged on His head and into the tangled locks of His hair. This done, my brother called the family and some disciples who were with us to join in pouring water over Him. One by one, we all poured water on Him while Babaji kept sat there like a statue. His body was completely still. It was like offering water to a Shivling.

Once His bath was over, my brother wiped the water off with a towel. The door of the bathroom opened, and He came out with my brother wearing a kurta with an *andi* slung over one shoulder. Mishrilalji, one of Babaji's devotees, had already prepared the *chandan*. This He applied on His forehead before doing the same for all of us. Thereafter, Babaji went back to His room to meditate. We learnt that He would emerge from His meditation at 8 a.m. to begin the yagna (fire ceremony).

The sacrificial fire-pit, called a havan kund, had been dug in the courtyard and preparations for the yagna began. Everything that would be needed had been pre-arranged. Devotees had told us that Babaji used milk and water in the yagna as offerings.

He came out of His room and sat on the *aasan* that had been placed for Him near the havan kund. The yagna commenced. He chanted mantras and made offerings of ghee and water. My brother and some devotees also followed suit. He completed the whole ritual in about half an hour, and then the kirtan began.

Thereafter, He sat in the veranda on an *aasan*, and devotees went to Him to place flowers and bel patra (*Aegle marmelos*), commonly offered to Lord Shiva, at His feet; they also showered some on His head. After giving darshan for an hour, Babaji retired to His room. I think my brother had taken Him in to offer Him some *bhog* of milk and prasad (made minus grains of any sort). The kirtans carried on.

I had been anxiously on the lookout for Chandramani, hoping to hear some more stories from him, and felt extremely disappointed when I discovered that he had not come to Bharatpur. Some devotees told me that being a mountain man, he had balked at the thought of dealing with the scorching heat of Rajasthan and had returned to Haidakhan with Babaji's permission.

Babaji emerged from His room half an hour later. The soothing sounds of the kirtan floated across the courtyard, creating a sense of harmony. The atmosphere was wonderful. It felt as if there was a wedding in our house. Around noon, the prasad that had been prepared for the devotees was offered to Babaji on a plate. He blessed it with His gaze (*Drishti bhog*) and sent it back to be mixed with the rest of the prasad. It was then distributed to all the devotees. A short while later, Babaji went back to His room to rest.

At four in the evening, Babaji was back at His *aasan*. Devotees started approaching Him for solutions to their various problems. The kirtan was still under way. One old lady told Him that she couldn't see anything. He asked a devotee standing close to Him to get some vibhuti (sacred ash made of burnt dried wood and offerings) from the havan kund. After it arrived in a bowl, He put some in her eyes. She started screaming. One disciple ran to her and helped her to sit down close by. After that, another person also complained of some pain in his eye. The process was repeated. Several people went to Babaji to have him put a pinch of vibhuti in their eyes as well. I noticed that He had covered His mouth with his *andi* and was quietly laughing while they wept.

Just then, my elder brother came and took me to Him. 'Babaji, this is my younger brother, Vijay,' he said.

Babaji smiled. He held my hand and put some vibhuti in my eyes too. I moaned as my eyes started hurting and it made me furious. After some fifteen odd minutes, I rinsed them and they finally started to open. I felt a new kind of energy in them. Shortly afterwards, the blind old woman announced that her eyesight had returned. It was a miracle! Babaji had put a little bit of vibhuti and bestowed vision on a pair of eyes that had no sight in them!

Everyone started swapping notes and exchanging stories about their experiences. His first day at Bharatpur ended with bhajans and kirtans; His second day too flew by in an atmosphere of intense spirituality.

Babaji was sitting on His *aasan.* It was around noon. I went to pay my respects. He grabbed my hand and put some vibhuti in my eyes again. I felt a searing pain and was livid, because I had not gone to Babaji to repeat the experience, and I had no eye problems. However, there wasn't much I could do in the circumstances. My eyes were still smarting, so walking away was not an option. Yielding to my fate, I gingerly sat beside His *aasan.*

A few minutes later, I felt a brightness behind my closed lids and the luminescence kept expanding. I felt as if the sun was coming out and destroying the darkness. The light was round in shape and I could see Babaji in it, with a snake and a ceremonial umbrella (*chhatra*) over His head. I screamed. Babaji immediately patted me thrice and uttered '*Om Shanti, Om Shanti, Om Shanti*', and the light vanished. I slowly opened my eyes, and at that moment it truly dawned on me that He was the Mahavatar Babaji Who had reincarnated for the good of the people.

Full of fear, my eyes opened completely. I looked at Him, and being prescient, He knew that I wanted to tell Him everything I had seen. He put a finger on His lips and forbade me from uttering a word. I said nothing. I was in no condition to be garrulous, but I felt both blessed and humbled. I was overwhelmed at the thought of having been bestowed with so singular an honour by Babaji. Just then, the *bhog* arrived. He blessed it with His gaze and left for His room.

Devotees were busy eating prasad. I still could not decide whether I should mention what had happened with me earlier to anyone. The evening came. Like every other day, after His bath, Babaji applied *chandan* on everyone. The kirtan went on, new devotees kept coming, and as long as Babaji remained in the verandah, none of them showed any signs of moving. His attraction was mesmeric; like a magnet pulling pieces of iron towards it. That night when I went to bed, I kept remembering how He had smiled at me whenever His gaze had met mine.

It was Babaji's third day in Bharatpur. A photographer had covered His entire stay. That day, he showed Him all the photographs and articles which had been published about Him in various newspapers. Babaji was to leave for Bandikui in the evening. The devotees who would be taking Him there had already arrived. There was a sense of sadness in the house, almost as if a bride was about to leave her home forever. My brother broke down while singing bhajans.

Shastriji told me that watching Babaji's farewell was extremely painful. Babaji had reincarnated to spread contentment on every inch of this earth, yet His departure always brought grief. The atmosphere at home was full of sorrow. Something infinitely precious to us was about to go away, and we would be left behind. The thought was unbearable.

His train was to depart at 6 p.m. Outstation devotees started preparing to leave. All of us stood with garlands for His send-off. The car which was to take Him to the station was standing outside, loaded with flowers. He came out of His room and everyone wept. My own tears would not stop flowing. No one wanted Him to leave, we all wanted Him to stay on. Some devotees lay in front of the car. Things were becoming that serious. There were sounds of weeping everywhere. Babaji was absolutely calm. What kind of avatar was this? He had no attachment to anyone—He was here today, there tomorrow. Everyone was attached to Him, and yet He was detached. This then was the true nature of God; He was above all worldly ties.

Babaji sat in the car. The wailing and screaming grew louder. That was when the true picture of love unfolded before me, and I thought this was how Lord Krishna's departure from Gokul to Mathura must have been, when the gopis had wept copiously, unable to endure the thought of their approaching separation from Him. Some had even given up their lives. This happens to devotees in every incarnation of God. Who wants to be left behind by Him? Yet in every incarnation, they fall prey to His obduracy and sacrifice.

It happened to Goddess Sati in the days when Lord Rama was separated from His beloved wife, Ma Sita, when She was abducted by the demon, Ravana. Almost mad with grief, He wandered with His brother Lakshmana through the Dandaka Forest, seeking Her in every nook and cranny, asking every leaf, flower and animal if they had seen Her.

Lord Shiva and His wife, Goddess Sati, were on their way back to Kailash after meeting the sage Agatsya. When Lord Shiva saw Rama roaming in the forest lamenting the loss of His wife, He bowed to Him. Goddess Sati could not understand why Lord Shiva was paying obeisance to an earthly king. Shiva explained that Rama was actually the avatar of Lord Vishnu. Goddess Sati did not believe Him and asked how this was possible when the king was weeping like a child over the loss of His wife. Lord Shiva replied that He was merely displaying the qualities of a human, as He was supposed to. Unconvinced, Sati decided to test Lord Rama. Her husband tried to dissuade Her but failed.

She appeared before Lord Rama in the guise of Ma Sita. Lord Rama immediately recognized Her and asked Her what She was doing in the forest alone. 'Where is Lord Shiva?' He asked. Ashamed, Sati returned to Her original form. But she was still not convinced. Sensing this, Lord Rama appeared to Her in His divine form along with Ma Sita. Her doubts gone, She bowed to Him and returned to Lord Shiva. However, knowing that She had appeared before Lord Rama in the guise of Ma Sita, Lord Shiva cast Her off, saying that He could no longer accept Her as His wife because He regarded Ma Sita as His mother.

This story has two morals: One, that despite being Lord Shiva's spouse, Goddess Sati had lacked faith in Him. Second, Lord Shiva's immense sacrifice—He left Ma Sati on the strength of one solitary incident. Lord Haidakhan had no attachments, because He was Lord Shiva in the flesh. How could any one ensnare Him in the superficial web of infatuations and illusions (*moh-maya*).

The train drew into the station. The whole place resounded with *jaikara* chanted by devotees; passengers peeped out of their compartments and felt blessed when they saw Babaji. He got into the train, and my brother with Him.

And what of the rest of us, the ones who stayed behind? We did what devotees have done through the ages: we went home with a heavy heart and wept.

16

OFF TO BANDIKUI

An overpowering scent of lotus flowers floated out from the room where Babaji had stayed in our house. I could hear the sound of kirtans echoing in my ears. We were all tired and went to bed quite early.

The next morning, I got up with an empty heart and went about my daily chores. My brother's family had already left for Bandikui. I was also thinking of going there, when a porter from the station came and said, 'Vijay Babu, your bhaisahib called on the railway phone from Bandikui. He wants you to go to the photographer and collect the photographs that he took of Babaji and take them to Bandikui with you in a day or two.'

I rushed to the photographer at full speed. In those days, there were no photo labs in Bharatpur. I told him to go to Agra and get the photographs developed quickly. He came the next evening and handed the entire lot to me. I decided to set out for Bandikui in the morning. Most of my family was already there.

I left for Bandikui in the morning by train. Babaji was staying at a garden retreat about 2 kilometres from the station, where the *Shrimad Devi Bhagwatam* was being recited and a Mahayagna was being performed for the Goddess Jagdamba. The Jhalani family owned the garden. There were five rooms and a well inside the compound. Babaji had one room, and His devotees occupied the rest. Shastriji was also there. He was the one who was reciting the *katha* (religious story). I reached the garden at 10 a.m. and bowed to Babaji before handing over the photographs to my elder brother.

17

TENSION AT BANDIKUI

Hari Shankar Bhatt, his younger brother Vishwambharji, and some devotees of Mahendra Maharajji had organized the Mahayagna in Bandikui. However, I discovered that most devotees were instead busy discussing Babaji's entry into town. Babaji had reached Bandikui at night, and a large assembly of followers had gathered at the station. The crowd was so huge that the station gate had accidentally broken in the ensuing melee.

Babaji had been seated in a buggy, and a massive procession followed Him through the town till it reached the Jhalanis' garden retreat, which was situated near the main market. There was a train line running close to the garden which went all the way to Agra. Hordes of devotees on incoming trains had happily pulled the chain to force a halt near the garden—so great was their haste to get Babaji's darshan. They descended from all directions, and their arrivals and departures were constant.

My stay at Bandikui was splendid. Once again, I did not feel like returning home. My elder brother noticed this but kept his counsel. He could see that I was getting immersed in the chants of '*Om Namah Shivay*' that were pervading the air.

Shri Vishnudutt Shastriji had taken to translating the Shrimad Devi Bhagwatam into Hindi for the benefit of devotees from 4 p.m. to 6 p.m. People would listen to his discourses intently. This would be followed by a kirtan, which would go on till about 9 p.m. Babaji would come outside and sit on His *aasan* during this period, spreading the lustre of His radiance on all the devotees. It was almost as if He had cast His luminescence over them. All of us remarked on it. Another extraordinary aspect of Babaji that we noticed was that He never needed to shave.

Babaji had been in Bandikui for four days when a Naga Baba went on the warpath against Him. He took exception to Babaji's decree forbidding all forms of addictive substances, including bidis in the compound. The Naga Baba had landed at the garden at around ten that morning and had started smoking a chillum stuffed with marijuana inside the premises. Several devotees requested him to go outside to smoke, as the place was a *yagyasthal* (the site where a fire sacrifice takes place), and a yagna dedicated to Goddess Jagdamba was going on.

The Naga Baba was incensed. 'What kind of joke is this! So much respect for one Baba and so much disrespect for another?'

He parked himself outside the compound and kept up a constant commentary, aimed at inciting public opinion against Babaji. He was joined by some like-minded disgruntled elements who were happy to support him. The atmosphere became tense. Babaji asked us to maintain calm. He said, 'Joy and sorrow are part of everyone's fate in this world. Today, the situation is such that where we are, there is great sorrow and where we're not, there is great joy!'

It is true that those that are bestowed with darkness are also given light. Just as a dark night is required for light, and a rose requires thorns to grow, in exactly the same way we need sorrow to spread fragrance in our lives. We need grief to understand life. Happiness will follow, thereafter. We all know that to touch a rose, one must get pierced by thorns.

Babaji was transcendent. He was pretending ignorance even though He was aware of everything. The number of people supporting the Naga Baba had grown, and they were raising slogans in protest. Anti-social elements had even started pelting stones from outside. Seeing the tension grow, devotees started fearing that something untoward would happen.

We are living in *Kalyug* when instead of walking the path of righteousness, people prefer to tread the path of iniquity. Only those who remember God through chanting and meditation are able to walk the path of virtue in *Kalyug*. The path of bhakti (devotional worship) may be strewn with thorns and is certainly a difficult road to follow, but its end is very sweet.

Throughout the day and that night, the supporters of the Naga Baba were unable to cross the boundary of the garden even though they wanted to. God knows what power prevented them from moving into the premises at night.

After the kirtan ended, Babaji went to rest in His room. Some devotees followed Him in. 'What's the matter?' Babaji asked. 'You all seem very frightened.'

The Lord of the Three Worlds was sitting there, but the faith of His followers had been shaken. They were hesitant to articulate the several threads of thoughts running through their heads, lest their wavering faith be revealed. It is also true that no devotee could get close to Him without His full benediction.

Mustering up a little courage they said timidly that Naga Baba's opposition had vitiated the atmosphere, hence, 'To avoid something untoward, we want you to leave this place with us.'

God always tests His devotees.

'How shall we go?' asked Babaji.

'We will make all the arrangements,' the devotees replied.

Babaji said 'Okay'. As the devotees turned to leave, He said, 'You can all go whenever you wish. We will not leave until the Mahayagna of the Goddess is complete, because the repercussions of an incomplete sacrifice are terrible and will cause immense destruction.'

Hearing Babaji's words, the devotees were filled with shame and fell at His feet, holding on to them. 'We are ignorant, and your heart is clear.'

Babaji's heart was pure, and why shouldn't it have been? When Bhrigu Rishi had kicked Lord Vishnu on the chest to wake Him up, the Lord had simply said, 'O Sadhu, did you get hurt?' Babaji's approach to His devotees was the same.

The noise outside had stopped. Perhaps the malevolent elements had gone home. We all went to lie down, but my sleep had vanished. I kept wondering what would happen on the morrow. Eventually, dawn crept through the darkness and pierced it with its light. Having completed their morning ablutions, all the devotees stood in a row waiting for Babaji to apply *chandan* on them. Thereafter, Babaji went in to meditate.

I came out as the sun began scattering its rays and wondered how the Naga Baba was faring. I saw that he was seated on his *aasan* with tears streaming down his face. He had fallen silent. There were three or four devotees sitting near him. It was almost time for Babaji to come out of mediation. By now, we were all wondering what kind of *leela* Babaji would unleash next. People had started collecting around the Naga Baba, but he was still silent. As soon as Babaji emerged from His room and sat on His *aasan*, the Naga Baba arose and started walking towards Him.

Babaji's devotees closed ranks and flanked Him protectively. A slow smile broke out on Babaji's face. The Naga Baba fell worshipfully on the ground and placed his head at His feet. He hit his head on the ground and wept. Having prostrated himself before Babaji, he refused to get up. Babaji's *leela* stunned us all. What kind of twist was this? How had it happened?

Babaji summoned two devotees and requested them to pick up the Naga Baba and bathe him. The Naga Baba started dancing in front of Babaji, and Babaji smiled. 'He is Batuk (the child form of Lord Shiva's assistant, Bhairava). Make sure you feed him a lot.'

In that instant, all Naga Baba's followers became Babaji's devotees.

18

BABAJI CURES A PARALYSED CHILD

After the dust had settled on the Naga Baba incident, a person came to Babaji with a child in his arms and placed him at His feet. The boy was paralysed. The child's father begged Babaji, 'Prabhu, save my child. I made a huge mistake.'

Lakshminarayanji and family, Chetramji, Chand Bihariji (my Mama, i.e., mother's brother), Mishrilalji, Lalji Ram Gopalji, Shastriji, Shri Harishankar (a devotee from Bandikui who was later conferred with the title of Pir by Babaji), his younger brother Vishwambharji, Shri N.K. Gupta, and a number of other people who had come from different parts of the country, were all present. Their gaze was trained on the child's father, who was repeatedly saying, 'Prabhu, save my child. You are Lord Shiva in the flesh. I made a mistake.'

Babaji smiled and comforted him with one hand, and a devotee asked, 'What on earth did you do?'

The man replied, 'My name is Ghasi Mali. I was with the people who were protesting here yesterday. I also threw stones with them. At night, I brought a black snake and left it near Babaji's room in the drain outside. We all thought that if Babaji was an incarnation of Lord Shiva, He would be safe from the snake, and if he was not, he would be exposed. I went home, but I kept feeling anxious and my anxiety would not let me sleep. I kept thinking "What have I done!"'

Quite often, a man's soul tries to stop him from wrongdoing, but he ignores his conscience and carries on with his misdeed, only to regret it afterwards.

He continued with his tale. 'My son was asleep when I went home last night, and this morning, I discovered that he had been struck with paralysis. I sent my brother to the *yagnasthal* and told him, "Go and see if Babaji has come out." My house is a kilometre from here. All sorts of thoughts were running through my mind, and I kept praying to God that nothing untoward had happened. My brother came back and told me, "Everything is fine there." I was frightened. I knew that my son has become paralysed today because of my bad karma. Lord, I have received the fruit of my karma. You are Lord Shiva in the flesh. Please show mercy on my child, and forgive me for my ignorance."'

Babaji was very compassionate. He melted at the anguish that had been publicly acknowledged and said softly, 'Go, take the vibhuti from the havan kund and apply it over his body. Your son will recover.' Lord Shiva is also known as 'Bhole Baba' (the simple one).

Still weeping, Ghasi reached the havan kund and rubbed the ash from it on his afflicted son's body. A miracle occurred, and Ghasi's child recovered completely.

In this country, people are unhappy when they see others happy and turn jealous of them. Just think, why did Ghasi Mali do what he did?

This incident has been depicted by a resident of Lohvan, Maheshji, in his hymn in Braj language.

सांप छोड़ और पत्थर फेंके, फिर आप ही आये बक्कारे जी ।
Saanp chhod aur pathar phenke, phir aap hi aaye bakkare ji **।**
गजब कर डारो या हैड़ियाखण्डी ने, जुलम कर डारे या भोले बाबा ने ॥
Gajab kar daro ya Haidykhandi ne, julm kar daro ya Bhole Baba ne **॥**

(After leaving a snake and throwing stones, he himself came and confessed. Haidakhandi performed a miracle and Bhole Baba forgave the one who sinned against Him.)

Word of Babaji's power spread in Bandikui and its surrounding areas. Thousands of devotees thronged to the garden to meet Him, hoping to improve their lives and solve the problems that dogged them. After nine days in Bandikui, Baba left for Jaipur. By then, the whole town had begun to recognize Babaji's *leelas*. '*Om Namah Shivay*' was being hummed everywhere. Babaji's miracles were discussed endlessly, and stories about them persist to this day. The news of His departure was received with sorrow. Wherever I looked, I saw tears. The bliss that His arrival had brought was equalled by the sorrow of His departure.

What kind of separation was this? We were all in the same boat. Shastriji always used to tell Him, 'Prabhu, I cannot bear being parted from you.'

Babaji was to take the evening train for Jaipur. All preparations were already in place and His farewell was a noisy affair. It felt as if all of Bandikui had converged to see Him off. His car set off for Jaipur amidst the chanting of *jaikara*. My brother went with Him, as usual, and I returned home to Bharatpur. I was filled with gloom. At the time, I was a student in class 9 and planned to take my class 10 examinations privately. I did not want to go to school, I no longer felt like staying at home. My mind was restless, it was pulling me to Babaji.

After hanging around listlessly at home for two days, I left for Jaipur. Babaji was staying close to the railway station in Bani Park, where an old Ram temple had a few rooms near its courtyard. There was a lot of empty space in front of the temple, where a huge platform with a throne-like chair had been built for Babaji. There were tents all around.

19

THE DIVINE PULL

The Mahayagna in Jaipur had been organized by Mahendra Maharajji's disciples. Prominent among them were Vaidya Mohanlalji and my Mamajis (mother's brothers), Shyam Bihari Gaurji and Chand Bihari Lalji. In one of the photographs taken at Bharatpur, Babaji has been captured standing, looking like the divine form of Lord Shiva.

On my first morning in Jaipur, I went for Babaji's darshan to His room. He looked at me and said, 'When did you come?'

'Last night, Prabhu,' I replied.

After applying *chandan* on my forehead, He said, 'This old man sitting here is your Guru. You must serve him well.'

I turned my gaze towards the gentleman who was sitting next to Maharaj. I saw a seventy-year-old man with a white beard. I was to learn later that he was Shri Govind Ballabh Pant, the priest of the Kathghariya Ashram. At that time, I had no idea who he was but nevertheless bowed to him and went out. After applying *chandan*, Babaji went into meditation and everyone left. My elderly Guru also stepped out of the room. I followed him.

My Mamaji was walking beside me. 'Who is he?' I asked him.

'He is the priest of the Kathghariya temple. His name is Govind Ballabh Pant. Kathghariya Ashram is in Nainital District and has a statue of Babaji in His previous avatar. Pantji has come from there. You had better serve him, since it is Babaji's order.'

I went to my Guru's room, and mindful of Babaji's decree, I kept asking him how I could serve him. I would finish all the tasks that he set for me and then go back for more. For five days, I waited on him day and night.

Each morning while applying *chandan*, Babaji would ask, 'Is Vijay serving you well?'

A pleased expression would flash on Pantji's face and he would reply, 'He's doing very well.'

Shastriji and the other devotees were also very happy with my conduct. That's when I learnt that Pantji was going back to Kathghariya Ashram and had issued an invitation to Babaji to attend the Ashwin (Autumn) Navratri there. Babaji had accepted.

Thousands of men and women were enthralled to see the divine form of God. All the deities invited by Babaji to the Mahayagna received the sacrificial offerings in their divine forms and returned to their world, satisfied.

From 4 a.m. onwards, Babaji would bestow His blessings by applying *chandan* on His devotees' forehead. People would return to their respective homes feeling empowered. Their sense of spirituality increased and they started feeling liberated from the miseries of life.

In Jaipur, Babaji would meet people between 2 to 4 p.m. People would converge to receive His blessings and would return happier. He would release His devotees from both physical and spiritual distress. The former, He would tackle at night before retiring.

Word spread, and He soon became a lodestone for the infirm. He not only treated ailing devotees but also the general public. People with all kinds of diseases would go to Him, and He would treat them by sprinkling vibhuti on their heads and putting three pinches of it in their mouth. They would go to Him in sickness and emerge completely cured.

Innumerable devotees welcomed Babaji into their homes, where they worshipped Him according to prescribed traditions. Several renowned siddha (enlightened) yogis and sages congregated for His darshan and declared they had achieved bliss.

Whenever Babaji went to a devotee's home, He would be welcomed with music played by bands that normally played at weddings. Devotees would also dance and sing kirtans for Him. Several of them had arrived in Jaipur from Delhi, chief among them being Chandra Singh Ranaji's family. Ranaji (later known as Swami Fakiranandji) requested Him to visit his residence in the national capital. Babaji agreed and later performed a yagna there.

Much later, a businessman from Calcutta (now Kolkata) came to visit the temple. He was very happy to see the havan kund and kept asking questions about it. Devotees told him that Lord Haidakhan had performed a yagna there during a visit. He subsequently built a beautiful temple at the *yagnasthal* (havan site) and dedicated it to Ma Jagdamba. He installed a statue of Ma Jagdamba and also made arrangements for *bhog*, service and prayers. This is how Sadguru Lord Haidakhan Baba inspired countless devotees to carry out myriad works of piety.

Babaji acquired a new devotee. His name was Amolak Jain and he lived in Bani Park, Jaipur. He once made a prediction about the future of the world, which is proving to be quite true today.

When Babaji prepared to leave for Vrindavan from Jaipur, He said, 'Vijay, we want you to stay with us for a few days.' I was in a fix. My affection for Babaji had been growing daily. My ties with home had been steadily weakening. I didn't know what to do. I lived with my elder brother Shivcharanji in Bharatpur. My mother lived in the village. My father had died when I was just twelve. It was the thought of leaving my mother and sister that formed the crux of my quandary. I did not worry much about my schooling, because I was taking my class 10 exams privately. I knew I could stay with Babaji and go home for my exams.

He seemed to sense my dilemma and, before I could say anything, He said, 'Go to Bharatpur and then come to Vrindavan.'

I had only been with Him for a very short time, yet I already knew that I did not want to leave Him. His latest direction was not just an order but also a great blessing for me, because I felt that I was the fortunate one. He was pulling me towards Him. I would be staying on, while the rest of His devotees in Jaipur would be bidding Him farewell.

He got into a car and was soon out of sight, leaving behind the splendour of His image with us.

One devotee approached me and said enviously, 'Vijay, how fortunate you are! Babaji has called you!'

I went to Vrindavan after seeking permission from my mother and brother and reached there at around 11 a.m. Babaji was sitting on His *aasan* and was very happy to see me. He smiled and said, 'It's good that you have come. Now you can stay with us for a while.' Thereafter, He proceeded to fuss over me, fanning me to chase away the heat, much to my immense embarrassment. He also saw to it that I ate properly.

My life with Babaji began. I stayed with Him as His constant companion, occasionally going home to take my exams, and with His grace, I passed each one of them without the slightest hurdle. This then was the start of my spiritual journey. My life had changed in the company of God.

20

A RUN-IN AT KHEDLI

One day, an old lady came to Vrindavan from Khedli Village in Alwar District to see Babaji. She requested Him to visit her village and give darshan to the devotees there. After Babaji accepted her invitation, she told Him that she would fix a date and inform Him. Shortly afterwards, she went back to Khedli to make the arrangements.

On the appointed date, Babaji reached Khedli with some followers. The old lady had informed her village that He was an incarnation of Lord Shiva, and a yagna had been organized. Lakshminarayanji and family, Acharya Shastriji, Chetramji, Mishri Lalji, Yashpal and a few other devotees from Bandikui and Jaipur were among those who had accompanied Babaji to the village. Accommodation had been organized for us at a public dharamshala. The old lady was already present there to receive Him. She was a member of the social trust which had made all the arrangements.

Khedli is famous for its wholesale grain market. The first day was spent singing bhajans and kirtans. On the morning of the second day, a huge yagna was conducted, followed by a massive *bhandara* (free food distributed as prasad of the deity) for the public. People had come from far and wide to see Babaji and participate in the religious sacrifice.

That night, Babaji sat on a platform in a large courtyard and devotees sang bhajans. Most were content to see Him in person. They were pleased that Lord Shiva Himself had been pleased to grace the world with His divine presence. Almost all of us were thrilled to achieve this ultimate bliss on earth, but as always, there are some ignorant people.

As the night progressed, Shastriji began his discourse. He told devotees about Babaji and how He had incarnated in human form. Some people interrupted him, and an argument broke out when they insisted that Babaji could not be an avatar. Matters had already become tense when a person brought a leprosy patient forward and presented him to Babaji. He looked at Babaji and said, 'If you are God, then fix him.'

Babaji said, 'We will fix him in three days.'

His challenger was unimpressed. 'In three days, you will kill him.'

Seeing the controversy getting out of hand, Prem Baba, a devotee of Mahendra Maharaj and a resident of Gokul, held up his trident and said, 'The Lord of the three worlds is sitting here in the village of Khedli today. I will bury alive each one who raises his voice against Him, right here and now.'

Babaji pacified him and told him to calm down.

The sky was clear. Babaji was gazing at it intently. All of us, His faithful devotees that is, had flanked Him as we normally did when a crisis brewed. We had dispatched indoors those women and children who had come from out of station. The crowd was getting aggressive, but Babaji did not move from His seat. Just then, some mischievous elements cut off the electricity at the dharamshala and we were all plunged into darkness. Ranaji and I rushed to tackle this new problem and found ourselves standing on the stairs holding various wires that had been deliberately snipped. Then, out of nowhere came a sudden downpour.

Babaji had obviously had enough of the miscreants and decided to display His divine powers. It was nothing short of a miracle. Just minutes ago, the stars had been shining brightly in the sky! It seemed as if Babaji had invited Megh Devta (the god of rain and thunder) for a flash dance. The heavy rains did the trick. People started running away and the *pandal* (huge tent) slowly emptied out. In the meanwhile, some locals informed the police of the quarrel.

By the time the police arrived, Babaji had already risen from His seat and had gone back to His room. When the cops knocked on His door, accompanied by a local magistrate, the room was already illuminated with the light of a stove that had been lit for the purpose. The magistrate asked Babaji why the fracas had broken out.

'We don't know,' He responded. 'We came here at the invitation of this old lady.'

The old lady was sitting nearby and crying. Babaji had been trying to soothe her.

The police asked Babaji about His future programme. Devotees informed the cops that Babaji would be proceeding to Rajgarh from Khedli in the morning. A senior police officer said, 'I am going to leave two policemen here for you. If there are any further problems of any kind, just inform us.'

The police party left with the magistrate; two cops stayed behind for our protection. The rain that had shown no signs of abating finally stopped at around 4 a.m. It had flooded the entire village, and grain worth crores of rupees had gone to waste. All outstation devotees left with their families that morning by train and other available modes of transport. The local public cursed the mischievous elements who had annoyed Babaji. They had all seen the terrible state of the market that day and harboured no doubts about Babaji's divine powers.

After a day's break in Rajgarh at Shastriji's house, Babaji returned to Vrindavan.

Sometime later, a delegation came to Vrindavan with the old lady from Khedli to apologize for the unfortunate incident. It not only comprised members of the grain market, but also the mischievous elements who had been the authors of the entire row and were now feeling regretful. They issued a fresh invitation to Babaji, asking Him to grace Khedli with His presence again. Babaji refused.

22

BABAJI EXPLAINS THE MEANING OF 'GURU'

Ramesh Bhai, a devotee from Bombay, asked Babaji why celebrations were held during Guru Purnima. Babaji, in His present incarnation, was not giving Guru Diksha (giving of a mantra or an initiation by a guru) to anyone. Nor did He make any disciples. His only mantra was: Truth, Simplicity, Love and the chanting of '*Om Namah Shivay*'. Nevertheless, He answered Ramesh Bhai.

'The word "Gu" means darkness and "Ru" means light; it means the light that destroys darkness. A person who destroys darkness with such light is a Guru. He teaches his disciples and monitors them. The disciple is the one who is tested by his Guru. He makes the Guru his master and offers him full devotion.'

He also said, 'We should not be influenced by the crowds around a person or by witnessing miracles. We should not choose gurus on such trivial premises. The full moon of the Ashadh month is called Guru Purnima. On this day, the disciple worships his Guru and follows his prayers with offerings.'

Babaji had explicated the concept of Guru Purnima so beautifully. His interpretation of 'Guru' too held us spellbound. Rameshji was not the only one who gave Him his full attention, we all did.

Babaji said that the person from whom we learn something becomes our Guru, and we should respect him. He said, 'People have a very narrow understanding of the meaning of Guru. A Guru is only regarded as a person who gives a mantra, which is not true. At birth, you first drink milk from your mother, so your mother is your first guru. Your father teaches you how to walk. We also learn a lot from our sisters and brothers. All of them are our gurus. But today, human ignorance has peaked, because we have forgotten all these things. This is why we stray, this is why we are not happy. A guru should be like the sun. Just as the sun provides energy to everyone, whether it is worshipped or not, a Guru too should be the same. That is why the sun is regarded as the primary Guru.'

Then he recited the couplet:

> '*Guru Brahma, Guru Vishnu, Guru Devo Maheshwaraha,*
> *Guru Sakshat, Parabrahma, Tasmaye Shree Guruve Namaha.*'

This Sanskrit shloka (couplet) dedicated to the Guru celebrates his wisdom and likens him to God. Babaji explained that the shloka equates the Guru to Lord Brahma the Creator, and like Brahma, the Guru creates us and generates the rites of worship and religion in us. The Guru is also compared to Lord Vishnu the Preserver, and like Him, the Guru nurtures our divine qualities. Finally, he is like Lord Shiva the Destroyer (transformer), and like Him, he destroys our desires and removes our flaws.

'The Guru,' said Babaji, 'is the true form of Brahman.'

Babaji was moving us from darkness towards light. He told us not to accept anyone as a guru, 'and if you do, then don't judge him, whatever he may be. The Guru will get the fruits of his karma, and you will get the rewards for yours.'

He put this into context with a story. It was about a rich old woman in search of a guru. She was very anxious, as she knew that there would be no deliverance for her without the intercession of a spiritual guide. A thief got wind of her search and kept a close watch. He was eyeing the old woman's wealth.

Each morning the woman went to a Shiva temple to offer water. The thief followed her there disguised as a sadhu. He sat down at a spot where he knew he would be visible and pretended to chant mantras using a necklace of rudraksha beads. When the woman emerged from the temple's sanctum sanctorum after making her offerings, she saw him and thought that God had blessed her with a guru in His own temple. Pleased, she approached him and said, 'I believe God has sent you to me. I request you to become my guru.'

The spurious monk pretended to refuse at first, but later agreed with a great show of reluctance. The old lady ushered him into her home respectfully and washed his feet, before performing an *aarti* to welcome him. She was ready to do anything to promote her newfound guru's happiness. The thief waited impatiently for an opportunity to steal her valuables. After dinner, the old woman took care of his sleeping arrangements. There had yet been no occasion to carry out any pilferage successfully, so he bided his time.

He found his chance the next morning when she went to a nearby well to fetch water for his bath. The thief trailed her. As soon as she reached the well and started drawing water, he pushed her in. The woman had her back towards him and did not know who had pushed her. She screamed, crying out, 'Guruji, help! Help!'

The thief ignored her cries, walked back to her house, tied all her valuables in a bundle and decamped. God, watching the entire proceedings, decided that though the old woman had made a mistake in selecting her guru, she had not erred in her strength of purpose.

There had been no lack of reverence in her devotion. He blinded the thief and forced him back to the well where the woman was still praying for her guru to come to her rescue. Carrying her bundled wealth on his head and now blinded, the thief heard the cries of the old lady and felt deeply ashamed.

Then God appeared in the guise of a shepherd, pulled the woman out from the well and told her, 'The man who you think is your guru is nothing but a common thief who was stealing your valuables.'

The old woman obviously did not realise that the shepherd was God said, 'I have surrendered all to my guru. That wealth belongs to him, he is free to take it. Who are you to come between my guru and me?'

God tried to reason with her, but she paid no heed. Her entire focus was now on her guru. She had finally noticed that he had gone blind. 'Guruji, what has happened to your eyes? They were fine earlier.' She began to wail. After a bit, she turned to the shepherd and said, 'I don't know who you are, but I know that you are no ordinary person. I pray to you to cure my guru's eyes.'

God was impressed. Though she had not chosen wisely, her reverence for the guru remained unchanged even after she had discovered he was a thief. Once she had accepted him as her guru, she had remained constant. The Lord assumed His original form and said, '*Tathastu* (As you wish/It shall be so)', and restored the thief's sight. The old woman then touched her guru's feet and said, 'If you had not shown your *leela*, I would not have had God's darshan. I am blessed to have you.'

Babaji concluded with the moral of the story—do not judge a person after you have made him your guru. Every word that Babaji uttered was like nectar to us. He did not speak much, but when He did, His words had a magic about them.

A short time later, Babaji went back to His room. I kept pondering over the tale He had told us long after He retired. It had touched my soul.

23

AT KATHGHARIYA ASHRAM

On 10 September 1971 we left for Haldwani by train. It left Mathura at around 11:30 p.m. Babaji and I had a first-class compartment, and thirty-five other followers from various places were in other compartments. We reached Haldwani at 9 a.m. the following morning.

Pantji was waiting at the station with a bevy of devotees to pick us up. A bus had been organized to ferry devotees to Kathghariya Ashram, and a jeep bedecked with flowers had been arranged for Babaji. It took the flower-laden jeep around half an hour to reach the ashram. The first thing that struck me about the ashram was its verdant serenity, enhanced by the flowers and shrubbery that grew helter-skelter all over the place. A cluster of trees shading it all added to its tranquility.

Several devotees had been stationed at the ashram to welcome Babaji on His arrival. As soon as He got off the jeep, He was greeted with chants of '*Bhole Baba ki Jai, Bhole Baba ki jai!*' He was subsequently ushered into a room and respectfully seated on a takht.

I reconnected with Pantji with a bow. 'It is nice to meet you,' he said while showing me to Babaji's room. 'This room is where Babaji will rest. The next room is for His *bhog*.' Having familiarized myself with the lay of the land, I brought Babaji's belongings to the room and started arranging them. Babaji did not eat or drink in public. In fact, plying him with food and water was an onerous task, as He would consume both like a statue.

Kathghariya Ashram is located on Kaladhungi Marg, seven kilometres from Haldwani and about a thousand yards from the main road. A beautiful verdant mountain stands about one-and-a-half kilometres away. Cascading down to Kathghariya from a waterfall in the mountain is a canal that fringes the ashram. It is about fifteen-feet wide and has been cemented. Its water is very clean. The temple area roughly spans fifty-three bighas (approximately nine acres). A huge circular platform built at the centre of the ashram circles large peepal, banyan and kadamb trees. The ashram was built by Babaji in His previous avatar. It is said that He used to sit near these trees in that incarnation, and it was here that He practiced His austerities for a long time. In those days, the area was thickly forested.

There is a Shivalaya in the ashram which has a Shivling that resembles the one at Kedareshwar. It also has a statue of the old Haidakhan Baba in His previous avatar, which was installed by Mahendra Baba. He established a second statue of the Old Baba in Vrindavan. During our visit, the ashram had tents for devotees, and a *bhandara* had been arranged for the day's meals.

A short while later, Babaji and I went for a bath to the waterfall accompanied by some devotees. After our ablutions, we returned to the ashram and Babaji sat on the takht outside His room. A small serving of the prasad prepared for devotees was taken to Him for *Drishti Bhog* so that it could be served to them. Having blessed it, He lifted His hand and told us to mix the serving with the prasad. After that, He withdrew to His room.

I had already reached the adjoining room with some seasonal juice and fruits, and now I fed these to Him before He proceeded for

His afternoon rest. Pantji had told me that Babaji would be staying at Kathghariya for a month and would attend the Ashwin Navratri functions here. Invitations had already been dispatched to devotees for the event.

At 4 p.m. Babaji came out of His room to mingle with devotees and asked them, 'How are you?'

What could they say? Except that they were in a state of ecstasy! As was His usual practice, He went to meditate from 5 to 7 p.m., after which He sat on an *aasan* placed under the trees surrounded by devotees, and an *aarti* was performed for Him. Pantji had organized a kirtan after the *aarti* and the entire ashram resounded with bhajans—'*Haidakhandi, Haidakhandi, Haidakhandi Bol! Samb Sadashiv, Samb Sadashiv, Samb Sadashiv Bol!*' Babaji blessed the devotees who had gathered around Him.

There was no electricity in the ashram, but provisions had been made for gas and lanterns. At around 9 p.m. Babaji went back to His room, and I brought Him a glass of milk. After drinking it, He handed the glass to me and said, 'Return it and come back here.'

When I came back, Babaji said, 'Get up at four in the morning, we will go for a bath. You can prepare the *chandan* thereafter.' Then He lay down on the mattress and covered himself with his *andi* (the sheet that normally hung over His shoulder). I started massaging His feet. A short while later, He told me He wanted to rest and I fell asleep on the ground with my head at His feet. I slept fitfully, because I was in a state of nervous anxiety. The flame of the *akhand jyot* (eternal flame) burnt dimly in the room.

Babaji shook my head gently at 4 a.m. 'Wake up Birju,' He said, addressing me by the nickname He had given me very soon after I started living with him.

I got up in a panic, bowed reverently to Babaji and headed out with my clothes. I walked towards the canal to bathe and attend to the call of nature. In half an hour, I was back in the room. Babaji was surrounded by devotees who were waiting to escort Him for a bath. I slipped inside, bowed to Babaji and then took out His clothes and a brass lota and handed these over to the devotees outside. In the three years that I served Him, I never saw Babaji going to the toilet. He always went directly for a bath. All the devotees who kept Him company were aware of this.

Once He left, I cleaned the room, ground the *chandan* and prepared everything. The Lord's *chandan* was prepared by mixing it with kumkum, camphor, saffron, etc. Babaji came back to the room while the devotees waited outside. I took out a comb and gently combed His hair. He applied some *chandan* on His forehead and then applied some on me. He did the same for the others as they went up to Him one by one. They touched His feet and left to meditate.

Early morning blessings from Babaji were highly prized. Devotees would get ready at three in the morning and sit outside Babaji's room to receive His blessings before they got busy with their day-to-day tasks. Babaji would then spend the next couple of hours in meditation. I would utilize this time to wash His clothes and heat milk for Him. At around 8 a.m., I would offer the milk to Babaji. He would barely drink half a glass. The remainder would be distributed to devotees as prasad. Prasad milk was like leftover nectar from Babaji.

As news of Baba Haidakhan's appearance began to spread, a fair number of devotees began to descend on Kathghariya Dham from various places. Babaji would emerge from His room at 9 a.m., give darshan to devotees, then go to the circular platform under the trees where devotees would anoint His feet with water and milk. This would be followed by an *aarti* and a kirtan. At 11 a.m. He would retire to His room and prasad would be distributed to the devotees. After resting, Babaji would come out again at 3 p.m. and participate in the activities for the remainder of the day.

Women devotees were particularly struck when they first beheld Babaji's beautiful visage. They considered themselves blessed and would keep marvelling over the way His form kept changing from moment to moment. Some of them declared that they had discovered the meaning of happiness in His presence. Each day, I blessed the good fortune which had given me the opportunity to serve the Lord. Undoubtedly, it was the result of my karma from a previous birth.

24

THE VERDICT

There was a stir in the mountains of Kumaon as word of Baba Haidakhan's appearance spread far and wide. Pantji felt blessed that he had found the Lord in his old age. He felt that his life had become meaningful. But there were others who forsook the path of truth and stood by falsity. Such people have existed in each age. Along with every incarnation of God, there have always been people born to oppose Him, like Ravana who clashed with Lord Rama, and Kansa who fought Lord Krishna. These are people whose inflated ego causes them to fall into the fallacy that they are greater than God.

Babaji displayed His *leela* in such a strange way at Kathghariya Dham that it became a talking point throughout Kumaon. The agricultural land belonging to Kathghariya Ashram had been illegally occupied by a member of the Legislative Assembly (MLA), Indra Lal, who regarded the property as his own. Pantji was extremely upset about the whole affair and harboured the hope that with Babaji's reappearance, the MLA would return the land to the ashram; but the landgrabber's mala fide intentions were soon in evidence.

A plea was moved in the magistrate's court alleging that a young man claiming to be an avatar of Haidakhan Baba, who had some devotees with him, was trying to take over possession of the ashram property. The plea demanded action against 'this person' and asked the administration to drive him out of the ashram along with his devotees.

On 13 September 1971, the Sub Divisional Magistrate (SDM) of Haldwani came to Kathghariya Ashram, accompanied by the Deputy Superintendent of Police (DSP), MLA Indra Lal and a posse of ten policemen. It was four in the afternoon and Babaji was meditating in His room. Panic broke out in the ashram at the sight of so many policemen. The police surrounded Babaji's room. I was petrified, fearing an untoward incident, and was trying to anticipate what would happen next when a policeman came up to me and asked, 'Is your name Vijay?'

I nodded and said, 'Yes.'

Having ascertained my identity, he said, 'Sahib wants to talk to you.'

I went with him to the SDM and was just in time to hear Ramkumar Sharma, editor of *Lok Sena Sandesh* of Jaipur, asking why the SDM had come to the ashram. Feeling awkward, I stood quietly, trying to efface myself as much as possible. The SDM replied that he was there because a case had been filed in his court by the local MLA, who alleged that a person posing as an incarnation of Haidakhan Baba wanted to grab property belonging to Kathghariya Ashram. He was there to question Babaji so that all doubts could be cleared and the matter resolved.

Ramkumar Sharma fell silent. The SDM then turned to me and said, 'Please tell Babaji that we are here to ask him a few questions.'

I entered Babaji's room fearfully. Spotting my nervousness immediately, Babaji asked, 'What's the matter Birju?' Babaji used to speak very little in those days, and His voice was very low-pitched.

I said, 'Prabhu! The SDM has come to ask you something. He is accompanied by a police officer and the local MLA, Indra Lal.'

'Spread the mat here and bring SDM sahib in,' Babaji instructed.

I silently laid out the mat and went out to request the SDM to come in. He trooped in with a police officer, the MLA, the tehsildar and one other person. They all sat on the mat that I had spread out. Babaji was still in mild meditation when the SDM asked me to close the door. He had stationed some cops outside. Barely sixteen at the time, I was scared to death and stood tearfully in one corner of the room with folded hands.

After some time, Babaji came out of meditation and opened His eyes. The SDM bowed to Him and said, 'I do not know who you are, but a suit has been brought against you in my court. It is in this regard that I need to ask you a few questions.'

I was afraid. I did not know whether Bhole Baba would even deign to answer any questions. Babaji looked at me and noticed that I was becoming a little emotional. He smiled at me reassuringly and then turned His attention to the SDM. 'Okay, ask.'

The SDM said, 'Maharaj, I don't mean to insult you, but the public has forced me into this position. Are you Haidakhan Baba?'

'Yes,' said Babaji.

The SDM asked, 'How are we to believe that you are Haidakhan Baba?'

Babaji said, 'Time will tell.'

'We cannot wait for Time,' remarked the SDM. 'You will have to give a statement regarding your identity.'

'We will give a statement,' replied Babaji.

The SDM then asked, 'Will you give us the statement here or in the court?'

Babaji said, 'We will give it in court.'

The SDM cautioned Him. 'Maharaj, I cannot offer the kind of dignity and respect you have here, in court. Therefore, I advise you to make your statement here.'

Babaji was unmoved. He said, 'SDM sahib, we will give our statement in court. You may treat us like an ordinary person there.'

The SDM shrugged and yielded. He rose and said, 'Maharaj, in that case, I will decide the date and time for you to come and make your statement.'

Baba assented politely and said, 'Please do.'

The SDM, who by then had thought the matter over, said, 'Come to court on Monday at 10 a.m.'

But Babaji had other plans. He said, 'SDM sahib, we will come to your court tomorrow.'

The SDM protested. 'Maharaj, the court does not open on Sunday.'

But Babaji was adamant. In the face of His stubbornness, the SDM capitulated in public interest, and because it was a prestigious case, or so he claimed. 'I will take special approval from the DM (District Magistrate), Nainital. You can come to court tomorrow morning at ten.'

The SDM bowed respectfully to Bababji and strode out of the room, with the others trailing him.

I was still standing near Babaji when He said, 'Go and see what the SDM is saying.'

Outside the room, the SDM was issuing instructions to the cops. 'Maharaj will make His statement in court tomorrow. Until we conclude the matter, you will not disturb any of His devotees.'

He left shortly afterwards, leaving the security of the ashram to seven of the police personnel he had brought with him. I went back to Babaji's room. He asked me what the SDM had said, and I recounted what I had heard. He heard me out intently without offering any comments.

The evening was upon us and His meditation time was over. The atmosphere outside was very tense. A few devotees were prey to all kinds of doubts, but most of them were saying, 'Everything will be fine, let tomorrow come.'

Things were back to normal once the *aarti* began. Babaji sat outside on His takht and people queued up to pay their respects one by one. I stood next to Him, collecting the offerings and garlands. Some devotees distributed these collected offerings to the public as prasad. Sounds of '*Om Namah Shivay*' and '*Haidakhandi, Haidakhandi Bol*' rent the air. Babaji went back to His room at 9 p.m. as usual, and I followed Him into the room with some milk. The rest of the devotees packed up for the night once prasad had been distributed. After drinking the glass of milk I had offered, Babaji said, 'Birju, we will go to court tomorrow. Talk to the devotees and ask them to make arrangements to accompany us.'

Later that night, after Babaji signalled that He wanted to rest, I lay on the ground and thought of the coming day. I wondered what would happen in court and felt a sliver of fear. 'God knows what will happen tomorrow,' I thought. I kept worrying and worrying until I finally fell asleep.

The next morning, when I returned from my bath, I found devotees swarming outside Babaji's room, waiting to take Him for His ablutions. I took out His clothes and handed them over to a devotee. Trying not to think, I tackled my morning chores and proceeded to complete them in a mechanical fashion. After I had finished cleaning His room, my attention was caught by the *akhand jyot* (eternal light). It was burning brightly and I felt a little reassured.

Shortly afterwards, Babaji returned from His bath with a bunch of devotees. They stood outside the room waiting for Him to apply *chandan* on them with lotus flowers. It's funny, but once the *chandan* was used to mark a *tripund* on their brows, I thought they resembled Lord Shiva's ganas (followers).

Babaji sat down to meditate. Remembering His instructions, I went up to the devotees and asked them what arrangements should be made for Babaji's visit to the court. Suggestions flew thick and fast, and we finally arrived at a consensus. We would take out a procession, Babaji would be seated on a buggy, and His devotees would lead the way with a band and a group of kirtan singers.

At 8 a.m., after Babaji had finished His meditation, I apprised Him of the devotees' plans and added that they were requesting permission to accompany Him in a procession and had made all the requisite arrangements. He acquiesced.

At 9 a.m. Babaji's procession started out from Kathghariya Dham for the Haldwani Court with chants of '*Om Namah Shivay*'. Slogans of '*Bhole Baba ki Jai*' and '*Muninder Bhagwan Ki Jai*' were also raised. Word had spread that He was heading to court to make a statement. The public had descended en masse on the streets, and all the thoroughfares were chock-a-block. Wherever I looked, I saw a sea of people. Devotees carrying fruits stood on either side of the road to receive Babaji's darshan and stopped us along the way to pay obeisance.

Babaji sat quietly in His carriage, occasionally raising His hands to bless devotees. Thousands had thronged to add to our numbers, some blowing conches, others showering Him with flowers. Several men and women had tears in their eyes. There were also those who were saying that today the truth would be known; either Lord Haidakhan would establish the truth, or He would go to jail. One set was convinced that Babaji would perform some kind of miracle. There were all kinds of emotions at play.

There was such a huge crowd in Haldwani that the cops had a tough time escorting Babaji into the courtroom. Police had been deployed all around the court premises. Only Ramkumar Sharma and I accompanied Him inside. All the others were stopped outside. Inside, dignitaries and prominent lawyers were present. Babaji was seated on a wooden chair on the dock. Ramkumar Sharma and I stood a short distance away.

The SDM left his chair and came down to Babaji. There was an expectant silence. The SDM gazed at Babaji for a moment and then said, 'Who are you? I don't know anything about you, so I request you to tell us something about yourself. I don't wish to arrive at a conclusion that I will regret for the rest of my life.'

Baba regarded the SDM in silence. The SDM repeated his request and added that that he didn't mean to insult Him by questioning Him but had no choice, as the public expected an answer. 'Are you Haidakhan Baba?'

'Yes,' said Babaji.

'What is your age?' Asked the SDM.

There was another silence.

'What is your age?' The SDM repeated the question, looking slightly annoyed.

Babaji calmly informed him that He would give him the answer the next day.

The SDM looked a little exasperated and said, 'Maharaj, you will have to answer me today, because we have organized a special court for you.'

'We will give you our answer tomorrow,' repeated Babaji, unyielding.

The SDM became angry and once again asked Babaji, more firmly this time. 'Maharaj, you have to answer the court, otherwise I will be forced to take legal action.'

Then, catching sight of me, the SDM said, 'Mr Vijay, tell Babaji that He has to reply today.'

Scared, I looked mutely at Babaji, not daring to say a word to Him.

Looking crosser by the minute, the SDM said, 'Maharaj, I give you fifteen minutes. After that, I will be forced to take legal action.'

Babaji broke His silence suddenly and said loudly, 'You can do what you like, but we will only give you our answer tomorrow.'

Babaji's declaration made the SDM nervous. He rang an iron bell that had been placed near him. A peon appeared. 'Get me a glass of water.'

The peon immediately brought water and placed it before him. The SDM then said, 'Get water for Babaji.'

Babaji refused to drink it. In any case, in the time that I had been with Him, I had not seen Babaji eat or drink anything in front of anyone. The SDM drank two glasses of water. There was perspiration on his face. The atmosphere was extremely tense as everyone awaited the SDM's decision. Babaji was still sitting in the chair that had been given to Him, looking very calm and relaxed. Wiping the perspiration from his face, the SDM finally announced, 'Maharaj will give His answer tomorrow. The court is adjourned till then.' He then told Babaji not to come with a crowd on the following day.

Babaji responded, 'We did not ask the crowd to come with us today, nor shall we do so tomorrow. The public was waiting for the court to make a decision with the hope that there would be a religious change in India.'

When Babaji came out of the court, thousands of people were still standing outside. Press reporters were hovering around, discussing the court proceedings. Babaji climbed onto the jeep that was waiting for Him and left for Kathghariya. After a while, devotees thronged the ashram and the place buzzed with discussion of the morning's events.

Many of them wondered why Babaji had refused to reply in court that day.

25

BABAJI GIVES US A SCARE

Babaji remained in His room for the rest of the day. I wondered why. At around 8 p.m. I went to Him. All of us had been waiting for His *leela* all day. The police were still stationed at the ashram.

He looked up when I entered His room and said, 'We have survived today. Who knows what will happen tomorrow? It's better to run away.'

I looked at Him completely aghast, unwilling to believe my ears. For a moment my mind went blank, and then I spoke, almost in tears. 'Lord, show me or them your *leela* now.'

He didn't seem to hear me. 'What are we?' He asked, 'What miracles can we perform?'

'Lord, you are everything,' I said.

He continued to scare me. 'In any case you have too much work. You'll be better off in jail.'

'Don't tease me,' I wailed and broke down.

But Babaji seemed to have gone deaf and was impervious to my tears. He kept saying, 'We will run away. The King of Nepal is our disciple. We'll take you with us through the mountains.'

My patience ran out. I started missing home. Had I left my house for this? I made an effort to control my mounting anger and tried to reason with Him. 'Maharaj, how will we run away from here? The police are all around us guarding the ashram.'

Baba waved away the small matter of the police and said, 'Don't worry about the police.'

I cannot describe what I felt at that time. I was outraged, angry, overwrought, yet determined to make Babaji do the right thing. I don't know from where I got the strength or the courage to challenge Him. But somehow, I did, and I dared to question Him. 'Lord, if you and I go away, have you even thought what the administration will do to your devotees who have come here from every imaginable place on this earth? What will happen to them? What will happen to the ashram? With what face will they tell the authorities where you have gone?'

Babaji conceded that I had a point. He said, 'Go! Ask the devotees what they want.'

It was almost 9 p.m. by now, and I ran to the devotees and told them that Babaji was calling them. I also told them that Babaji was saying that He was Nothing. Thoroughly frightened, they all went with me to Babaji's room and prayed to Him to come up with a miracle that would resolve the controversy.

Babaji said, 'Who are we to perform miracles? We cannot do anything now.'

For the next couple of hours, devotees repeatedly pleaded with Him to show them His *leela* and render them fearless. They told Him that they believed He was Lord Shiva in the flesh. The more daring among them even said, 'We won't be able to show our faces if you leave. People will say, you believed that He was God, look what He turned out to be!' But Babaji was still in denial and persisted in turning a deaf ear to their pleas. It was almost 11 p.m., but devotees kept on praying to Babaji in every possible way they could devise. Several broke down.

Perhaps it was their doggedness, but Babaji suddenly changed tack and said, 'Why are you so worried? If there is *kaal* (time) in this world, we are *Mahakaal.* We have 1 crore 34 lakh ganas (followers) in Uttarakhand alone. Who can touch us? If anyone dares, one word from us and they will eat him alive. Forget the SDM, there is no power in the world that can do anything to us.'

He then uttered the words '*Om Shanti*' thrice and then said '*Vishram*!' (Rest). At that instant, we felt His power pervading the room. It empowered His devotees and, overcome with delight, they started shouting, '*Bhole Baba ki jai.*'

After paying obeisance to Babaji, the devotees trooped out of the room. Babaji had won them over with His words. But I was still unsure as I shut the door after them. Even though I had felt His power just moments ago, I could not forget what He had suggested earlier. Babaji had said such a big thing, and I was still not sure what He would do eventually.

Babaji lay down. He asked me to retire for the night as well. I was too scared to sleep, fearing that Babaji would disappear while I napped. I tossed and turned restlessly throughout the night. At four in the morning, Babaji shook my head and asked me to get up. I was already up. I picked up my clothes and surreptitiously hid the lock of the room, with its key, between them. I then bowed to Babaji and went out. I locked the door from outside, turning the key slowly so that I would not be heard. By now, I had worked myself up into quite a frenzy and was afraid that Babaji would take off while I was bathing!

I took the quickest bath of my life, ignoring the other devotees who had turned up at the canal. Once I was done, I cornered some of them and asked them to oversee Babaji's ablutions. They came along to His room with me. Other devotees were already outside. I opened the lock covertly and again hid it between my clothes. As I stepped in, I saw Babaji was in meditation.

After He returned from His bath, Babaji applied *chandan* on all the devotees in the room and then went into meditation again.

At 8 a.m. sharp, I went to Him with some milk, and after He drank it, I asked Him what time He wanted to reach the court and by what mode of transport. Babaji asked me to arrange a jeep. 'We don't want too many people to go to court with us. We will leave at 9:30 a.m. from here.'

I bowed and went out to make the necessary arrangements. The jeep arrived at the ashram at 9 a.m. Pantji, as ashram priest of Kathghariya, was trying to maintain calm and telling the devotees at the ashram not to panic.

I informed Babaji that the jeep was ready. He said, 'Only you and two or three others will go with us.'

26

BABAJI TRIUMPHS

Babaji sat in the jeep, and Ramkumar Sharma and I clambered in. En route, we saw hundreds of people marching towards Haldwani. Everywhere there were chants of '*Bhole Baba ki Jai*'.

When we reached Haldwani, we saw that the public had assembled in even greater numbers than the day before. People were sure that the moment of truth would arrive that day. Babaji entered the court before the clock struck ten and sat on the same chair He had occupied the previous day. The police had been deployed in full force and there was an air of suppressed excitement inside the courtroom too.

The SDM rose from his chair and went to Babaji and said, 'I request you again not to think that I am insulting you. I am questioning you on public demand.'

Babaji inclined His head graciously, without speaking.

The SDM shot his first question of the day at Babaji. 'How old are you?'

'131 years,' replied Babaji calmly.

There were murmurs of surprise that soon died out when the SDM voiced his next query. 'Where are your parents?'

'We have no parents,' said Babaji.

The SDM then asked Him about the status of His education. Babaji informed him that He had none. The SDM rephrased his question. 'What is the level of your knowledge?'

'We have knowledge of the four Vedas,' said Babaji.

There was a short pause, then the SDM said, 'The complainant has alleged that you also have a wife and children.'

Babaji rubbished the charge. 'We have neither a wife nor any children. If they exist, tell the complainant to bring them in front of us.'

The SDM then asked, 'Maharaj, how did you acquire the disputed land?'

It was a question that linked Babaji to the Old Haidakhan Baba.

Babaji proceeded to explain.

He said that in the middle of the land, which now belonged to His ashram, there was a cluster formed by huge peepal, banyan and kadamb trees. 'We were doing penance there in 1922. In those days, the area was heavily forested. The British commissioner of Nainital and his wife were wandering in the woods and came upon us. He told us that his wife and he did not have any children and prayed to us to bless them with a child. We gave them our blessing. After some time, a son was born to them. He came to us after the birth of his son and said, "Maharaj, by your grace we now have a child, and my wife and I would like serve you in some way. Please let me know of some service that I can perform for you."'

Babaji told the court that He had smiled at the commissioner and said, 'We want some land for an ashram here.' He said that the commissioner had immediately issued orders, asking his subordinates to investigate the status of the land, and over time had allotted thirty-five bighas of land to Him.

The SDM interrupted Babaji at this point. 'But the land over which Maharaj is in dispute is fifty-three bighas. Where did the rest of the land come from?'

'The villagers gave us the rest of the land,' replied Babaji.

The court then studied the land records and found that Babaji's entire statement was indeed true.

The party that had filed the case was unable to counter this and made no response.

The SDM pronounced, 'We believe that you are Haidakhan Baba. If the opposing party does not agree, it should provide proof.'

27

BHOLE BABA KI JAI!

People waiting anxiously for the verdict outside erupted in cheers as soon as it became known. Celebrations broke out. All of Haldwani reverberated with chants of '*Bhole Baba ki Jai*'. The atmosphere at the ashram was jubilant. Drums were beaten and people converged to Kathghariya Ashram from all directions.

Babaji, however, had had enough. After returning from court, He retreated into His room to rest. Devotees kept questioning me about the courtroom drama and I happily narrated the whole tale, telling them how boldly Babaji had responded in court. At around 3 p.m., some journalists came to the ashram and approached Pantji saying, 'We want to talk to Babaji about today's incident in court.'

Pantji replied that Babaji was resting, 'You will have to wait.' He then called out to me and, introducing me to them, said, 'Vijay, when Babaji gets up, please take these people to Him.'

One journalist took charge of the formalities. 'My name is Padmadutt Pant,' he announced. 'I am from *Sandesh Sagar*. This is Lalit Kishore Pandey, he is from *Uttarayan* newspaper.'

The duo were accompanied by a bank manager who appeared to be a devotee and also bore the surname Pandey. Soon after, I went to

Babaji and found him sitting quietly on His *aasan*, lost in thought. I gave Him some water and waited until He had finished drinking it. Then I told Him there were some journalists outside wanting to meet Him.

He was silent for a moment and finally sighed and said, 'Call them in.'

I brought the journalists into the room and shut the door. Bank manager Pandey had also come in with them.

The journalists opened attack almost immediately. 'You have hurt the religious sentiments of the people by claiming that you are Haidakhan Baba. There is massive confusion among the public. You have hurt the faith of religious people with all this scandal. If you are the same Haidakhan Baba whose miracles are well known, then show us some miracles too.'

Caught up in his diatribe, *Sandesh Sagar*'s Padmadutt Pant was not ready to listen to anything Babaji had to say. He did all the talking himself. 'If you are Baba Haidakhan, then you should perform some miracles, so that the faith that the public has lost is restored and the sadhus who are accusing you of hypocrisy are silenced.'

Babaji finally managed to get a word in. 'Keep faith. Everything will be alright.'

I was thoroughly annoyed by Padmadutt Pant's behaviour but kept my mouth shut. He continued to insist that he wanted to know the truth about Babaji. 'When I go from here, my article will be your inspiration rather than mine. If you do not tell me the truth about yourself, I will give up my life right here at your feet.'

Baba reiterated that he should be patient. 'Everything will be revealed in time,' He said. But Pantji had started hitting his head.

I noticed Babaji's face turning red with anger. He shut His eyes, and suddenly Padmadutt Pant screamed and cried out, '*Bas kariye Maharaj* (Please stop Maharaj!)' and fled the room and the ashram and was seen running in the direction of Haldwani.

His screams had scared us all. It had shaken his two companions to the point that they quickly bowed to Babaji and beat a hasty retreat. As I escorted them out of the room, I was accosted by the overpowering sight of an immense gathering waiting patiently for Babaji's darshan. I went back to the room to apprise Babaji of the latest situation. I noticed that His eyes were still red and quailed at the task at hand but, nevertheless, manfully broke the news to Him. He did not look particularly pleased but indicated that He was ready to give darshan.

The queue was endless and devotees started trickling into the room one by one. I stationed myself at one end of Babaji's seat while Chetram stood at the other, and we set aside the garlands and fruits offered to Him. The line of devotees remained unbroken even after two hours. We finally called a halt and told the rest of the devotees to wait outside, as it was time for Babaji's bath. He resumed giving darshan after His ablutions and then it was time for His meditation.

That night, He did not come out of His room. When I went to Him with a glass of warm milk, He remarked that He didn't know why people came in search of miracles only to run off when they saw one. He then indicated that He wanted to rest. I nodded and left Him in peace. I also lay down on the ground and fell asleep almost immediately. It was a peaceful and welcome slumber, and Babaji woke me up the next morning.

The day started with the usual round of chores. Preparations for the Mahayagna for Navaratri had begun at Kathghariya. Devotees from Rajasthan, Uttar Pradesh and Bombay were coming for the festival. Arrangements were being made in schools to lodge outstation devotees. Locals came forward to assist in the groundwork for the Mahayagna. Ghee, sugar, money and all kinds of provisions had started pouring in. Babaji refused to touch the money and asked me to handle it. Pantji was exultant as he saw the ashram prospering.

In the midst of all these arrangements, I spotted journalist Padmadutt Pant. He had come to Pantji, the ashram priest, with a bundle of newspapers. Babaji was in meditation at that time. I was sitting next to Pantji when Padmadutt greeted him. The elderly priest smiled and teased him gently. 'What did you think of Babaji's miracle?'

Padmadutt blinked and hung his head in shame. He said he wanted to meet Babaji, so I went to Babaji's room and saw He had risen from meditation. He smiled slightly and I asked, 'Did I do something wrong yesterday? You've been very angry since last evening.'

'No, Birju,' He said, 'What's the situation outside?'

I informed Him of Padmadutt Pant's presence. 'He's waiting outside with a bundle of newspapers. He wants to meet you.'

'Show him in,' said Babaji.

The newspaper man entered the room with the ashram's priest, looking very tentative. He flattened himself at Babaji's feet and started sobbing. Babaji tried to calm him. 'Get up, Pantji. These things happen.'

I helped him to his feet, but his tears wouldn't stop. He placed the bundle of newspapers at Babaji's feet and went back to Haldwani. I opened the bundle and took out a newspaper. Babaji said, 'Tell us what it says.'

I started reading Pantji's article aloud. It was full of the rise of Haidakhan Baba. A huge smile broke out on Babaji's face. I could see that He was hugely entertained. I must say that it was quite riveting. It began with the following words: 'The appearance of the ever-young, immortal form of Shiva, Bhagwan Haidakhanwale Baba, has a special message for the people.'

Padmadutt Pant narrated his initial encounter with Babaji and admitted that at the outset, he had believed that Babaji was a '*seedha pahari ladka*' (simple mountain boy) in the clutches of an unscrupulous group of people who wanted to present him as Haidakhan Baba to con the public. He described what he had seen when Babaji had shut His eyes:

> I told Babaji forcefully that I would only go after I learnt the truth; that what my pen wrote would be inspired by him and not me. Tell us the truth, I said. At this point, Babaji shut His eyes. After that, what I saw is indescribable. When I saw a radiant many-headed deity, I became soaked in sweat and tears began to flow from my eyes, and I said, '*Bas kariye Maharaj*!' (Please Stop, Maharaj!) I opened the door and came out. Based on what I witnessed and experienced, I am giving His message—'*Bhav Rakho* (Keep Faith)'.

Babaji was extremely entertained and once again remarked that He did not understand why people wanted to see miracles when they couldn't withstand the sight of them. Soon it was time for Babaji to meet the public. I accompanied Him out of the room and distributed copies of the newspaper among the devotees, who devoured the article eagerly.

Kirtan began after the day's work. Many outstation devotees had arrived that day, including Lakshminarayanji and his family, Shraddhanandji, Phoolchand Tiwari, Shri Amolak Chand Jain and a large number of devotees from Jaipur, devotees from Bandikui, Natthi Lal Vaidya of Delhi, Nanakchand Guptaji, Shyambihari Gaurji, Chandbihariji, Mohanlal Vaidyaji, and my mother and brother Shivcharanji with his family.

They all cornered me and questioned me about the court case. Ashwin Navaratri was scheduled to begin four days later. Shri Vishnudutt Shastriji was due to arrive the next day. We all believed that the Goddess Saraswati spoke through him. There was an influx of local devotees, and as the dispute had been resolved, the SDM finally decided to dispense with police presence in the ashram. He, however, left two policemen behind for security.

Thanks to the local dailies, news of Babaji's appearance spread like wild fire through the entire region of Kumaon and also percolated across to the rest of the country. It opened the floodgates. Suddenly, we were inundated with devotees from all parts of India, and people of all religious denominations started visiting the ashram. Residents of Haldwani also converged in large numbers and there was a definite hum in the air.

28

THERE IS SORROW IN ATTACHMENT

Preparations for the Navratri festival were in full swing. Shri Vishnudutt Shastri came from Rajgarh, and as soon as he arrived, he bowed reverently to Babaji. The recitation of the Shrimad Devi Bhagwatam was to be carried out under his supervision. Babaji was in His room at the time and devotees were flocking in to pay their respects—my mother and my brother among them.

My mother tried to garland Babaji. He stopped her and said, 'You have not come for us, you have come to see your son. Garland him.' I was standing right next to Him, and I could see the tears in her eyes. I asked her to garland Babaji. I was aware of her sentiments; no mother wants her son to be an ascetic.

That evening, Babaji came to the ashram grounds and sat down. An *aasan* was being made for Shastriji to sit on while reciting the Srimad Devi Bhagwatam Katha. There was a joyous air all around. At 9 p.m. Babaji returned to His room and lay down. I started pressing His feet. Babaji said, 'Your mother has come to see you.'

I said, 'Maharaj, Mother has given birth to me. She has an attachment for me, but I am not as attached to her.'

Babaji laughed and said, 'There is always sorrow in attachment. We will tell you a story.' I listened to Him with rapt attention while pressing His feet.

Babaji began his tale. 'Once upon a time, there was a king and a queen. The queen used to bathe the king daily. One day while giving him a bath, the queen suddenly laughed out loud.'

Curious, the king asked, 'What is the matter? Why are you laughing?'

But the queen would not tell him. The king, who was as stubborn as he was inquisitive, persisted and asked once again, 'Tell me, O Queen, why did you laugh today?'

She still kept her silence and the king became even more eager to learn why she had laughed. After much perseverance, he managed to break down her resistance, and she replied, 'Dear king, my sister who lives in another state will give you the answer to this question.'

The king went to his sister-in-law the next day. The queen's sister gavc thc king a rousing welcome and asked him the reason for his visit. The king replied, 'Your sister bathes me every day. Yesterday, while bathing me, she started laughing loudly. When I asked her why, she said, "Dear king! My sister will answer your question." I have come here to find the answer.'

The queen's sister said, 'I will definitely answer your question, but before I do, I have a condition. Whatever I tell you must remain between you and I. You have to promise me this, because I have knowledge of my past life. I also know how far I have to travel in my body in this world.'

The king said, 'Devi, I promise you that what you say to me will remain between you and I.'

Reassured, the king's sister-in-law said, 'Listen, dear king! I'm pregnant. I will give birth to a baby boy tonight. After giving birth to the child, I will abandon this body and will be born as a girl in another state. After some time, this boy born from my womb will marry me. Today I will be his mother, in future I will be his wife.'

The king was surprised at her words. Noticing this, she told him, 'I cannot violate the norms of decorum, O king. When I leave that kingdom after marriage in my next life, I will answer your question.' With this caveat, the king's sister-in-law went inside the palace.

The king was deeply puzzled and kept pondering over what she had said. That night, his sister-in-law gave birth to a son. An hour after his birth, she left her body. At this turn of events, the king thought, 'Well, this has come true.' Sometime later, he discovered that a girl had been born in another state. The king returned to his own palace with a sad heart.

Many years passed, and the time came for his nephew's marriage. The king had been eagerly waiting for the event for several years, and he went for the nuptials enthusiastically. The wedding was celebrated with great pomp, and finally the moment of reckoning arrived and the bride's palanquin left the palace. On the way, the king stopped the palanquin. 'Do you recognize me?' He asked the princess.

Without batting an eyelid, she said, 'Yes.'

The king then asked, 'O princess! What is the answer to my question? I have waited so many years, and I am very anxious for your response!'

The princess smiled at him and said, 'Dear king! How is it that you haven't found the answer to your question till today? You have seen that the boy born from my womb is taking me as his wife. I have told you as much in the past as well. This is the law of destiny! Listen, O king! The wife you have today was your mother in a former life. When she bathes you, she sees you in the childlike form of your past life and laughs at God's *leela*.'

Horrified by what the princess had told him, the king lost his bearings. He abandoned everything and walked towards the forest.

I had been listening very closely to Babaji's tale. After it was over, He said, 'Birju, let us give you knowledge of your previous birth.'

I panicked and said, 'No, God, I do not need any knowledge. I just want to grace your feet.'

Babaji said, 'Son, the biggest sorrow always lies in attachment.' He smiled, and I kept wondering why He had told me this particular story.

Babaji went to sleep. But I kept turning the tale over in my mind till I too fell into a deep slumber.

When Babaji woke me up me up in the morning, my mind was still reeling from the tale He had told me the night before. Strange thoughts filled my head and I started speculating about my previous life. What had I been in that life? What connection, if any, did the story have with my last life?

By then, Babajii was ready for His bath. I thought perhaps I'd ask Him about my last life after He returned. By the time He came back, it was timc for Him to apply *chandan* on devotees. After that, he sat down to meditate.

I went out to the ashram grounds to help in the preparations for the yagna, and the moment passed. My questions remained unasked.

29

MAHAYAGNA

It was almost as if I had been split into two. I was helping out with the preparations for the yagna and yet simultaneously keeping a hawk-like eye on Babaji's room care to ensure that no one went anywhere close to it, lest they disturbed His meditation.

Hundreds of devotees were arriving at Kathghariya Dham. Eminent personalities of Haldwani had also started coming to the ashram. Today was the first day of the yagna. Babaji offered ghee in the yagna with a group of devotes. Several scholars were chanting mantras. The recitation of the Shrimad Devi Bhagwatam text began traditionally. Babaji only went to His room at noon, after the full sacrifice of the yagna had been completed.

After that, work began at the *bhandara* and prasad was distributed. It continued till 4 p.m. Thereafter, Shastriji began to read aloud from the holy book, translating Sanskrit into Hindi. All the devotees had gathered around to listen to his discourse. It set the trend for the next nine days. Devotees would collect around Shastriji each evening to listen to his recitals attentively. Babaji too would sit under the cluster of trees to listen to him.

Among those who religiously attended Shastriji's discourses were Shri Trilok Singh (later known as Maha Muniraj), Paramhansji, Amar Singh Yadav, Ramprakash Bhasin, Ramesh Bhatt the Chairman, Pratap Singh the Sarpanch, Kushal Singh, and Matadin Gupta.

After returning to His room on the first day of the yagna, Babaji asked me to put some fruits, cashewnuts and raisins on a plate, and keep Rs 10,000 in my pocket. Then He told me to bring Trilok Singh. The two had never met. His actual words were: 'There's a man in a white pant-shirt sitting next to a Baba at the back. Go and bring him here.'

Trilok Singh had taken to coming to the ashram regularly with Paramhans Baba. He would generally pay his respects, attend the bhajan, kirtans and Shastriji's discourses, and float around the ashram without making any attempt to put himself forward. I found him sitting next to Paramhansji and asked him to come with me. 'Babaji wants to meet you,' I told him.

He got up and followed me to Babaji's room. I opened the door gently and entered inside with my companion. Babaji ordered me to shut the door. Trilok Singhji bowed to Babaji and sat near His takht. 'Lord, what are your orders for me?' He asked.

Babaji smiled and signalled at me. I put the fruits and nuts in front of him and Babaji instructed him to take the prasad. He respectfully complied. Babaji then asked me to hand over the money to him. I quietly handed the wad of notes. Babaji said, 'This is a wad of ten thousand, take it and use it for all the arrangements here. Bring ghee, vegetables, sugar and other provisions to the ashram. We can do the accounts later.'

The magnitude of the task that he had been entrusted with pleased Trilokji. But he was also astonished.

I was equally astounded when he told Babaji, 'Maharaj, my name is Trilok Singh. I have a shop at Patel Chowk in Haldwani called

Hind Grain Traders.' Trilok Singh, it turned out, was one of the biggest grain and grocery merchants in Haldwani.

I stared at Babaji, amazed. How had He known? How had He picked the right person out of so many people? How had He known who could be trusted with the responsibility of arranging provisions for the ashram? Even today, I marvel over it. But somehow, He always knew how to sift the dross from the gold. He could always separate a true devotee from those who were faking devotion. In my own case, I never moved a step without His guidance. He steered me in the direction He thought best for me and kept telling me what to do from time to time, and if that were not enough, He would also often tell me how it was to be done.

Babaji smiled at our amazement and then changed the subject. He turned to me and said, 'This is your elder brother. You will call him bhaisahib from today.'

After Babaji had finished with us, I went to see Trilok Singhji off. On our way out, I introduced him to some outstation devotees. I also told Laxminarayanji and Chetramji that Babaji had chosen him to oversee all the arrangements and that he was a resident of Haldwani.

Trilok Singhji went back to Haldwani, and I went back to Babaji's room. 'Your bhaisahib has gone,' He observed. It was a statement, not a question.

'Yes,' I replied. How could anything be hidden from Lord Shiva? He could even permeate an atom.

The Mahayagna celebrations continued and the number of visitors to the ashram grew daily. The tale of Haidakhan Baba's appearance had now exploded all over Kumaon. At that time, there were two more saints in the area. One was Nantin Maharaj, and the other was Neem Karoli Baba. Nantin Baba used to wander from place to place in the mountains. Many of his disciples lived around Haldwani and were mostly prosperous. Many of them came to Kathghariya Ashram to see Babaji. They had apparently asked Nantin Maharaj whether the sage who had come to Kathghariya was Haidakhan Baba. He had smiled and avoided a direct reply; he however directed them to come to Babaji for darshan.

Neem Karoli Baba had an ashram at Kainchi Dham near Bhowali. He was a worshipper of Hanumanji.

During the Mahayagna, the Kathghariya Ashram priest, Pantji, brought several people to Babaji, among them an old woman accompanied by a man. Presenting the old lady, he said, 'Maharaj, this is Durga Devi, Dr Hemchand Joshi's wife. Dr Joshi was your devotee, and this is Dr Bindu, a very renowned doctor. They have come from Almora.' Both of them touched Lord Haidakhan's feet.

Overcome by the sight of Babaji, Durga Devi said, 'If my husband were alive today, how happy he would be! Our life was blessed.' She folded her hands and continued, 'Babaji Maharaj! My husband wrote a book about you in 1965, and at the end of that book, he prayed that it should be dedicated at your feet and that you should get it printed. Prabhu, now that you have appeared, you can fulfil my husband's last wish.'

Babaji blessed her and said, 'We will definitely get this book printed. Bring it when you come next.'

The main copy of the hand-written manuscript was with the tehsildar of Pithoragarh. After much effort, the book was procured from him. It was titled *My Dear Lord Haidyakhandi*.

A few words on Dr Joshi are necessary here. Dr Hemchand Joshi was a resident of Almora. He wrote this book in 1965, after being directed to do so by Shri Mahendra Maharaj. Dr Joshi was one of the greatest linguists ever. He was a renowned name among eminent scholars, not just in India but around the world. He had undertaken research for fourteen years while residing in Europe, especially in France and Germany. He had also made a mark in the newspaper world, having worked as editor of daily newspapers like *Calcutta*

News, Vishwamitra, Bharat Mitra, etc. He also produced many texts on linguistics.

The last lines of page 103 of Dr Joshi's book were prescient enough to astound Babaji's devotees. In it, he had written: 'Lord, I dedicate this book at your feet. When you appear, please have it published yourself, and after it is published, I will make an offering of a temple bell weighing 50 kg.' He concluded the dedication with: '*Tvadiyangranth hey eesh, tumbya mev samarpev.*' (All religious texts in this universe belong to You, O Lord, I give unto You what is Yours.)

Dr Joshi died five years before Babaji appeared, but ever-sensitive to His devotee's sentiments, Babaji took the book from Durga Devi and had it printed. After its publication, Durga Devi fulfilled her husband's pledge and made an offering of a huge temple bell weighing 50 kg to Babaji. It hangs at the Haidakhan Temple to this day.

In the meanwhile, devotees were pouring in from all over the country. Babaji's miracles were being hotly discussed. I considered myself very lucky. I had always wanted the whole world to know about Babaji. I wanted them to see Him and salvage their lives. Each day, after the havan was over, Babaji would visit various devotees at their homes in Haldwani. Trilok Singhji too requested Babaji to grace his house, an invitation that He accepted graciously.

At about 1 p.m., one afternoon, Babaji and some of His followers went to Trilok Singhji's house at Haldwani. It was situated in a lane near the Bholanath Bageecha (garden) and was very beautiful. A lovely temple stood in the middle of the edifice. Babaji was escorted and seated in one of the upper rooms and an *aarti* was performed for Him.

Trilok Singhji's children were young at that time. Only two of his daughters, Shanti Behenji and Maya, were married at the time, both into distinguished families. The remaining seven children, comprising three girls and four boys, were then too young for matrimony. Trilok Singhji's wife enveloped me in kindness. She often declared that she felt the same affection for me that she did for her own children. That day, Babaji returned to Kathghariya Dham at 3 p.m. after the offerings and *bhog*. It was the fourth day of the Jagadamba Mahayagna.

Later, one night, Babaji suddenly said to me, 'Son, we will not come to this ashram again.'

I was surprised. 'Prabhu, you have so much here. Why is your love for this place ebbing away?'

He smiled and said, 'You should always abandon a place where there is a dispute. Renunciation is the biggest ornament of man. People here should not think that Baba came here to grab land. We will make many such ashrams. Do not worry. But keep this to yourself. We are not attached to anything. Why should we fall in love with this ashram?'

He was true to His word. In the following fourteen years of my life with Him, He did not go to Kathghariya Ashram again. Till date, the managers of the ashram have been repeatedly requesting the Haidakhan Trust to take over the ashram, but as Babaji did not heed their pleas in the past, the trust too has chosen to honour Babaji's wishes.

On the fifth day of the Mahayagna, people from many provinces reached Kathghariya Dham to participate in the full sacrifice of the yagna. Devotees were dropping into the ashram from morning till evening. Stories of Babaji's miracles had spread far and wide. He was making offerings of water after ghee during the yagna. The wishes of devotees were being fulfilled at the mere sight of Him. Everyone was getting what they wanted.

Purnahuti (the completion sacrifice) took place on the ninth day of Mahayagna. After that, a huge *bhandara* was organized. This part of my story concludes with the recitation of the Srimad Bhagwatam on the ninth day.

30

A BRUSH WITH DEATH

After a month in Kathghariya Dham, Babaji had decided that it was time to head to Haidakhan. Outstation devotees began to leave, as the Mahayagna was over. Vishnudutt Shastriji was planning to return home to Rajgarh on Dussehra. My mother too was going back with my brother. She had tears in her eyes, probably because she could see that she was losing me.

Four days after the Mahayagna, Babaji said, 'Tomorrow morning we will go to Haidakhan. Make all the necessary preparations.' When the Kathghariya priest, Pantji, learnt of our plans, he became teary-eyed. I could see that parting with Babaji would be hard on him.

I had been told that Haidakhan Dham was about twenty-two kilometres away from Kathghariya, and one could only get there by foot, as there were no other means of transportation. By morning all our preparations were complete. Some of Babaji's devotees had reached Haldwani by bus and jeep and would be walking with us up the mountain path.

We set out for Haidakhan Mahadham, accompanied by a procession of about a hundred devotees. We would undertake a ten-kilometre climb up the mountain to reach a mud track which transected a plateau and then sloped downwards, or so I had been told. Our luggage had been loaded on horses. A Sikh devotee volunteered to drop some of our goods on his Massey Ferguson tractor. It was so crammed that a sack of flour had to be tied to the tractor's bonnet, as all the space in the back was already taken.

Along the way, Babaji and I distributed boondi prasad from a bucket to passers-by; the tractor crawled at a snail's pace behind us. I was so engrossed with the task at hand that I failed to see a small stone in front of me and stumbled and fell. The bucket of prasad slipped from my hand and rolled away, and I went sprawling flat on the ground. The front wheels of the tractor, which had been right behind me, went over both my legs. It came to a screeching halt as I screamed. The driver had not seen me fall because of the sack of flour on the bonnet.

At the sound of my screams, a stampede ensued. Babaji came to me with some devotees and said, 'Birju, get up.'

I was weeping and cried out, 'Prabhu, my legs have been cut.'

Babaji smiled. The serenity on His face calmed me. 'Get up! Your legs have not been cut.'

I stood up slowly with Babaji's support. I could feel the strength of His arms. They were like pillars. I felt a slight pain in my legs and winced. There was a hut nearby that doubled as a tea shop. Bit by bit, Babaji gently took me there. The devotees around us were getting nervous.

Once I had been seated, Babaji said, 'Birju, let us send you to a hospital.'

I shook my head. 'No, Lord, why should I go to a hospital when I have you?'

Babaji smiled before turning to the tea shop owner. 'Bring me some mustard oil.'

The owner brought the oil and handed it to Babaji, who started applying it on the backs of my knees.

I said, 'Lord, you must not do this!' How could I let Babaji touch my legs? He paid no heed to me. And as soon as Lord Shiva in the form of Babaji touched my legs, my pain disappeared.

Baba then asked for a horse. When it came, He said, 'Birju, sit on this horse.'

'Prabhu, I will not sit on a horse while you walk.'

He looked stern. 'This is our order.' I instantly obeyed and gingerly mounted the horse.

Babaji walked beside me. After we had covered a short distance, He asked me, 'Are you in pain?'

I shook my head. 'No, Prabhu.'

His next words stunned me. 'Birju, if you had been somewhere else today, you would have died. Today was the day of your death.' I looked at Him speechlessly. Other devotees walking alongside also heard Him. He had granted life to a nobody like me! What could be a greater miracle than this?

31

A NIGHT HALT

My mind was awhirl! How could I possibly give milk and fruits to Babaji without bathing? Babaji seemed to have read my thoughts. He smiled and said that in the mountains, a man could be clean without a bath, as the air was filled with purity.

We had halted for the night in Ukhaldunga village at Ram Singhji's house, which fell on our way. It was about 7 p.m. by then. The days were now short, and dusk had already fallen. Ram Singhji, a very mild and virtuous person, welcomed Babaji reverently into his house. He was a teacher. He had a Plaster-of-Paris idol of Prabhu in the temple in his house. Ram Singhji was the first person to have taken a photograph of Babaji performing his austerities at Mount Adi Kailash, which stands above the cave of Haidakhan.

Ram Singhji had made meticulous arrangements for our food and lodging, and I ensured that I was allowed to stay near Babaji's room. After *aarti*, everyone touched His feet, and Babaji called for an end to the evening once prasad had been distributed. 'We will leave for Haidakhan from here at seven in the morning,' He announced.

Our host took milk and fruits for Babaji's *bhog*. I was with Him at the time and after sipping some of the milk, He gave it to me and said, 'Add some turmeric and drink it.'

I did as I was told and was then ordered to sleep. Babaji woke me up in the morning before going for His bath. I bowed down to Him, gathered His clothes and handed them to Ram Singhji. Before leaving, Babaji issued stern instructions to me: 'You are not to bathe for three days.'

I was appalled. 'Babaji, I have to prepare the *chandan*,' I protested.

'It doesn't matter,' He said, 'prepare it without bathing.'

After His bath, Babaji chanted mantras with all the local devotees and then sat in meditation. In the meanwhile, preparations for the onward journey had begun. Haidakhan Dham was still about 12 kilometres away. Our ascent had ended at Ukhaldunga. We would now be descending all the way to Haidakhan. The devotees left after breakfast, taking care to thank Ram Singhji for his hospitality. We also headed out soon after, bidding Ram Singhji's family a fond farewell.

32

HAIDAKHAN AT LAST

Ram Singhji went to Haidakhan with us. I was still on horseback. Babaji kept stopping every now and then to ask me how I was feeling. At 11 a.m. we reached Haidakhan Vishwa Mahadham. I got off the horse. Babaji held my hand. As soon as I felt His touch, my body started vibrating and a strange feeling washed over me. I could feel all my pain vanishing, and I knew that I was cured. Babaji had performed yet another miracle!

Chandramaniji, who had regaled us with so many tales of Babaji's miracles in Vrindavan, was also present at Haidakhan. We entered the temple through a small footpath. There was a small Shivalaya (Shiva temple) in the middle. Babaji told us that the Shivling inside was about 200 years old and resembled the one at Kedareshwar. There were big stone pillars around the temple and a hut in front, which had a *dhuni* (make-shift fire pit that sadhus dig to protect themselves from the cold); inside it lay a trident (*trishul*) and a pair of tongs (*chimta*). On the northern side of the temple was a stone and cement platform about seven feet long, two feet wide and eight inches high. A mat had been spread over it. Babaji sat on this platform facing a havan kund that had turned a deep grey with years of smoke. Locals from Haidakhan Village had also arrived for Babaji's darshan and were bowing to Him.

There were three rooms made of stone, mud and dung on one side at the back. Two of them were on the ground floor and the third room was on the floor above. I took our stuff (Babaji's and mine) to the room upstairs. Babaji had already plied me with instructions. 'Birju, you will be in the room upstairs, and the others will be in the lower rooms. The women will stay in one room, and the men can take the other.'

There was no electricity in the ashram. I noticed that there was a takht in the room. I plonked our food provisions on one side and carefully placed Babaji's clothes on the other. Chandramani had brought milk from his house in an aluminum bucket. I used three bricks to build a make-shift stove behind the rooms below and fed it with wood to heat some milk for Babaji. Then I carried the warm milk to the room upstairs, informing Him on the way that His milk was ready.

Babaji was still downstars, seated at the *dhuni* near the temple (this was where He would sleep for a long time to come). After a while, He came upstairs and I handed the milk to Him and then fed Him raisins and cashews with my own hands. I still remember how I felt at that time. There was a strange thrill and honour in knowing that I fed The One who feeds the whole world, the One whose *leela* even the gods are eager to witness; and here I was feeding that Narayan with my own hands. It was such a privilege!

Khichdi (dish made with rice and lentils) had been made as prasad for devotees on that first day. Once we had finished eating this simple fare, I was finally free to absorb the view. I realized that it was even more beautiful than Chandramani's description of it in Vrindavan. There were huge mountains in the northeast in front of the Haidakhan Vishwa Mahadham Ashram. People told me that Nar and Narayan had meditated on one of the mountain tops, and

Lord Shiva had stopped overnight at the other mountain—the Chota Kailash—on His return after marrying Sati.

The river Gautami Ganga was just about 100 yards away from the temple and could be reached via a crude footpath. Everyone went there for their ablutions and to answer the calls of nature. Across the river was the Haidakhan cave, and above it, the Adi Kailash. Locals said that the river derived its name from the sage Gautam, who is said to have performed penance there. The Gautami Ganga gushed through boulders creating a half-kilometre-long channel between the temple and cave. What an amazing place it was! Bhagwan Haidakhanwale Baba's temple had huge peepal trees inside its complex at the ashram. Their size revealed that they were very old.

At around 4 p.m. Babaji decided to go for a bath. I walked down with Him to the river. Some followers came along too. I carried His clothes and brass *kamandal* (a water pot used by ascetics). We spotted an elderly man coming from the riverside and Babaji hailed him, 'Govardhan Singh, come here.'

The gentleman bowed to Babaji, and they walked towards the Gautami Ganga together. There, Babaji took off His clothes on the banks of the river and waded into the water. Once He had put some distance between us, He went supine and started floating. He kept drifting with the flow of the water, not moving His hands and feet, not even to keep balanced while afloat. It was a sublime, stunning sight; only an extraordinary being could stay so still on a moving water-surface. I became lost in the wonder of His latest *leela*.

After fifteen minutes, He came out of the river. I wiped His body with a towel and helped Him put on a fresh set of clothes. As He walked up to the temple, He asked me to fetch some water in the *kamandal*, which He then offered to the Shivling in the temple. I, in the meanwhile, went off to wash His clothes.

The priest of the Shiva temple at Haidakhan Dham was Paramanandji, who hailed from a nearby village. On that first evening, he began with a regular temple *aarti* and followed it with one that was dedicated to Babaji. He was very old. Babaji asked me to give him some clothes. I brought a dhoti kurta from the room and gave it to Babaji, who handed them to the priest.

A fire had been ignited in the *dhuni*, and some devotees were sitting near it while others sat outside. A kirtan of '*Om Namah Shivay*' was underway. Babaji was sitting in meditation. At 8 p.m. Babaji ordered everyone to retire for the night. He expected all of us to be up and ready for a bath in the river at four in the morning. His instructions for me were slightly different. 'You have to get up at three in the morning, take a bath and clean the temple. Make sure you also clean the *dhuni*.' He covered Himself with *andi* and went to sleep.

I went up to the room and found I could not sleep, because I was in a panic. The place was taking a toll on me, but I did not dare breathe a word about it to anyone. What an effect it was having on me! At 3 a.m. sharp my eyes flew open and I dutifully walked towards the Gautami Ganga with my clothes and bucket. The air was icy even though it was only October. I wondered what it would be like in the dead of winter.

I shivered as I stripped and entered the river. My body became numb as soon as I immersed myself in the freezing water. I scrambled out of its frosty embrace as fast as I could and sat down on a boulder with a towel wrapped around me. There was a fast-moving breeze, and there wasn't a soul in sight. All of a sudden, I felt an intense wave of nostalgia for my home in Bharatpur. A short while later, having donned a fresh set of clothes, I started climbing up with a bucket of water.

Today there are 108 steps from the top to the Gautami Ganga, and it is difficult to traverse the distance even when there is nothing to carry. But at that time, Babaji had imbued me with so much power that I used to come up with two buckets of water at a time using the footpath.

Babaji was already in meditation. I took out a fresh set of clothes for Him and handed them to some devotees who were already there waiting to accompany Him. He proceeded towards the river, and I started preparing the *chandan*. There were days in winter when the *chandan* would literally scrape the skin off my palms. But I would carry on doggedly, determined to do my best for Babaji. I would clean the temple, light a lamp and apply a paste of mud and dung on the *dhuni*.

By around six every morning, Babaji would sit upright on His *kushaasan* (a seat or mat made of kusha grass) and ignite the fire in the *dhuni* for a small havan. He would make offerings of ghee and other items. The light of the flames in the havan kund would fall on His forehead and illuminate His entire body till it shone like gold, increasing the wonder of His beauty manifold. The havan would be followed by an *aarti*, and it was only after it was over that we felt free to turn to chores that were part of our daily routine.

At nine in the morning, on our first day at Haidakhan, Babaji said, 'Birju, let us show you the cave', and I walked to the cave with Babaji and some devotees. There were several streams flowing into the Gautami Ganga. Babaji predicted: 'You will see, one day the number of people who come to Haidakhan will equal the number of stones that are here. There will be a constant flow of people from all parts of the world.'

And I thought, 'God knows when that will happen. There isn't even any proper place to live.' But knowing Babaji as I did, I knew that His words would come to pass. He was a great being, and if there was a God somewhere in this world, He lived in the venerable Haidakhan Baba. Babaji could solve the greatest problems in a matter of seconds. 'It will definitely happen,' I thought to myself, 'but when?'

Babaji interrupted my thoughts, and I realized that we had reached the cave.

'Birju,' He said, 'this is where we came from. It goes into Nepal all the way to Mount Kailash.' I bowed before the sacred cave. He sat there, soaking in the atmosphere for a while and suddenly said, 'We will build temples here too.'

Nobody had ever envisioned that a temple could be built there. But Babaji, barely a day after returning to Haidakhan, was already teeming with ideas. I could see that His resolve was stiffening, and I knew that once He had made up His mind, He would make things happen. There would be a temple there. And there eventually were—nine of them!

Babaji decided to stay on in Haidakhan for the time being. First of all, He had boundary walls built around the temple. Devotees of Lord Haidakhan would come to see His world on foot, making the twenty-two-kilometre-long trek to reach Him. Food came on horses from Haldwani, as did the cement. There was a community kitchen, and all the devotees would get together to cook the prasad. It was only made once a day. Meals were eaten together and prasad was distributed. Devotees would line up all the way to the Gautami Ganga to send water up to the temple. At that time, even utensils had to be carted down to the river for cleaning.

I was very fond of drinking tea. Laxminarayanji had brought a light stove from Haldwani, on which I used to heat milk for Babaji. Chandramaniji used to bring milk and curd from his house every morning at eight for Babaji. His village was about 3 kilometres from Haidakhan. Chandramaniji had also developed a great affection for me over time and would spend hours describing the days that he had spent with Babaji.

During this period, Babaji used to give darshan round the clock—sometimes at the *dhuni*, sometimes outside, and sometimes near the wall that was under construction. It was a time when Babaji was always on the move, walking around flinging instructions at artisans.

He kept stressing the importance of karma and demonstrated this in a number of ways. Wood was used for offerings and cooking prasad; the requirement grew rapidly as the number of devotees visiting the Dham mounted by leaps and bounds. Sometimes, He would go down to the river, pick up the massive logs floating on it and carry them all the way up on His shoulders.

This had a huge impact on devotees and proved to be the perfect cure for slackers. Offenders guilty of indolence would instantly get energized into action, while the more conscientious among the disciples would try to prevent Him from picking up the logs. 'Why are you carrying wood when we are here?' They would ask.

Pat would come the reply, 'How can we ask you to do something, if we are not willing to do it ourself?' His words would effectively reduce everyone to either silence or shame, depending on how hard they had been working.

Some devotees were curious about His food habits and asked Him why He did not eat grains. He laughed and said, 'We will one day, when the time is right.'

In the early days, when there was paucity of accommodation at the ashram, people would sleep on sheets at the *parikrama sthal* (circumambulatory path/area around the sanctum sanctorum) of the temple. Babaji would tell His devotees beforehand how much prasad they needed to make each day. His estimates were never wrong, and new visitors would discover that He was an *antaryami* (omniscient one) when meals were served.

He displayed His prescience in other ways too. Sometimes, He would mention incidents that He said had taken place in the outside world. His predictions would be borne out a few days later, when the newspapers (always a few days old) would be delivered to the ashram. The newspapers were always highly prized items and eagerly awaited—even when we were not trying to check out Babaji's statements—because they formed a tenuous link for us with the world outside.

Time went by. Sometimes, while bathing in the Ganges in the morning, it used to get so cold that I would miss home. Babaji always knew and would smile and say, 'Birju is missing home.' I would laugh in response, and He would remark, 'Worry is like a pyre.'

As always, He was right. When I think of Babaji today, I remember His many kindnesses to me. I never even suffered from a fever or cough while I was with Him. The life that lay ahead of me, I owed to Him, because as He had said while we were on our way to Haidakhan, 'If you were somewhere else today, you would have died.'

Today, I am proud to write that if there is a God somewhere, He existed in Haidakhanwale Baba, whom we all saw in the flesh. There are images of Lord Ram and Lord Shiva that we carry in our heads. But I have never met a person who could pinpoint Lord Haidakhan's form or claim 'I have seen Him; this is what He was like.'

He was an '*ajanubahu*' (a person whose hands reach his knees; one of the thirty-two signs in Hinduism which typically mark a man as a God, Saint or a King). The shape of His neck was like a Shivling, His body emanated the fragrance of *chandan*. He had all the qualities which define divinity, and all the *kalas* (qualities, gifts and graces) that we expect in God.

33

STORM IN A TEA CUP

One day Baba said, 'Birju, quit tea.'

I do not know why I loved tea so much. At that time, there was a tea shop in Haidakhan, about twenty furlongs from the temple, and there was no other store of any kind in the village. The tea shop was run by a man named Chandan Singh, who is still there. His father Govardhanji used to come to Babaji. The fields that ran alongside the temple belonged to two gentlemen, Harak Singh and Khadak Singh. Babaji gradually bought the land from them and had the ashram constructed.

I often used to go to Chandan Singh's shop to have tea when Babaji went to bathe in the evenings. There were several occasions when saints would visit Haidakhan Ashram. I would cook food for them. Preparing food is an important ritual in the mountains and forms an important part of the culture there. Women cook food with purity. During their menstrual cycles, they avoid the kitchen. Complete cleanliness is maintained. Scholars say the mind becomes whatever you eat. Mahendra Maharajji used to tell his devotees that sisters should never be angry while cooking, as it passes on to the person who eats it. Anger vexes the intellect, it seeps into your dough.

One day, Babaji suddenly came into the room upstairs when I was making tea for myself. As soon as He entered, I tried to hide the teapot under the takht.

Babaji spotted it and said sharply, 'What is in that pot?'

I folded my hands and said, 'Tea.'

He said, 'You have not quit tea, yet?'

I shook my head nervously.

As He left the room to return to the *dhuni*, He said, 'Tomorrow we will go to Surya Devi, where we will get you to quit tea.'

I did not utter a word. I was full of remorse by then. And dread. What awful means would Babaji devise to cure me of the habit? There was also an element of self-flagellation. Why had I tried to conceal the tea from Babaji when I believed that nothing could be hidden from Him?

Babaji came back to the room that evening and I offered Him milk, which He accepted. As stated earlier, He used to consume fruits, milk, fruit juice, potatoes, some nuts, cashew nuts, raisins and sometimes vegetables, but refused to touch grains of any kind. Babaji had fresh instructions for me. 'Look, we will go to Surya Devi at eight in the morning. Pack clothes for two days. There is a saint there whom we want to meet. Keep a shawl and some sweets and nuts for him. Place them in front of him with Rs 101 when we tell you to.'

I bowed, relieved that He was still talking to me.

After Babaji left, I started packing. I put all His things in a big bag and my own in a separate case. I placed Babaji's gifts for the sadhu in a small bag. Exempted from my daily chores in the morning, I made preparations for our departure. There were not many outstation devotees at the ashram at that time. Just before we left, Babaji told His disciples, 'We are going for two days. Make yourself comfortable here.'

34

MY CUP OF TEA

Chandan Singh's father Govardhan Singhji, who must have been around sixty years old, was waiting for us along with another man. When Babaji saw them, He said, 'Let's go!' and promptly asked me to fetch our luggage. When I brought down both our bags, Babaji told me to hand them over to Govardhanji's companion. I hung on to a sling bag, which contained some fruits, drinking water, Babaji's steel lutiya (small vessel for drinking water) and a few other items.

We set out from the ashram towards the mountains facing us. Babaji had taken a big stick along, and Govardhanji led the way. Govardhanji's companion and I followed them. It was the start of a slow climb across four mountains.

'Birju,' said Babaji, 'a good saint lives where we are going. We are taking you there for darshan and to help you quit tea. It is a very beautiful place. Remember one thing: if the saint respectfully asks you to enter his hut, you must go inside. One must always go where there is respect. Never go to a place where there's a possibility of insult.'

When I remember the truth of Babaji's words today, I become emotional. He was like a father teaching His son, moment by moment, all the things He thought were worth knowing. He was

God, but He taught me how to observe decorum and uphold dignity, not only my own but also everyone else's. He always said that there must be humility in charity. 'Always be humble while giving away something you own. Never do it out of pride or to show the world, otherwise the value of the gift becomes meaningless.'

Surya Devi Baba's abode was at a distance of about ten kilometres from Haidakhan. The entire route was covered with forests. After a climb of some four kilometres, a part of the path ran down the mountain. How can I describe the joy of walking with Him who ran the whole world? After a while, as I looked down, I noticed that one of His toes was bleeding. A mild scream escaped my lips.

'What's the matter?' Asked Babaji.

I pointed towards His toe and said, 'Prabhu, your toe is bleeding.'

'It doesn't matter,' He said dismissively.

I paid no heed. 'No, Prabhu. Let me tie a strip of cloth around it.'

He laughed and placed His toe in the ashes of a burnt tree nearby. As soon as He pulled His foot out, I noticed that the bleeding had stopped. We resumed our trek through the jungle, and He said, 'One of our devotees is undergoing an operation in Bombay today. There was a shortage of blood, so we had to donate some.'

I said 'Oh, okay, Prabhu,' acting as though I understood.

It was only later that the reason why He had bled actually sunk in. I found out that Vora sahib—an ardent devotee of Babaji—had indeed been undergoing an operation in Bombay at that time. When I recounted Babaji's *leela* to some devotees afterwards, they were unsurprised. 'It's all His grace. What can He not do?'

After walking for five hours, we reached our destination located in the middle of wilderness. There was a settlement about four kilometres away. Babaji pointed out a natural carving of a goddess on a mountain rock. A stream trickled below it. It had come from the mountains and was flowing downwards. 'That,' He said, 'is Surya Devi.'

There were two huts in front of the cave that housed the temple. One hut was at a lower level while the other stood around four feet above it. Babaji asked us to settle ourselves in the lower hut with our luggage. 'Come up when the Baba calls you.'

He went to the hut above. We heard a voice yelling, '*Eeja*, *Eeja*!' It sounded as if someone was crying. I asked Govardhanji what *Eeja* meant. '*Eeja* means mother, in the mountains,' he replied. We fell silent.

A short while later, Babaji came down. 'Come for a bath,' He said and headed towards the flowing waterfall. I followed with His clothes and lota. There was a tall tree nearby. Babaji had climbed onto it and was plucking some fruits that were shaped like black kernels. He came down and broke them with a stone. Noticing my curiosity, He said, 'It's the custom here to wash one's hair with these fruits.'

He crushed the fruits enough to produce foam and applied that on His head as He stood beneath the waterfall. Thereafter, He put on fresh clothes and walked back to the upper hut. I washed His clothes in the waterfall and dried them outside near the lower hut. I was still sitting there when I caught sight of Surya Devi Baba for the first time. It was almost seven in the evening. I saw him walking down to us from the hut above. He said, 'Vijay, you live with Him Whom I call Mother. You are now everything to me. Come up.'

I bowed and followed him to the hut above. Mindful of my instructions from Babaji, as soon as he sat down, I presented him with a shawl and placed it at his feet, along with Rs 101. Babaji was in meditation. A *dhuni* was burning brightly. There was silence all around, broken only by the sound of running water.

After some time, the sage looked at me and said, 'Look, Vijay, I have been living in this forest in the shelter of Surya Devi for thirteen years. I accepted water from Eeja's (Babaji's) hands a year ago. Today, I want you to make tea for me with your own hands.'

There was a mud stove behind the hut. I noticed that he had everything that was needed in his abode. Babaji cut in, 'We brought him here to make him quit tea, not to drink it.'

Surya Devi Baba turned to Babaji and said, 'Let him accept tea from sadhus and mahatmas. Ban him from drinking it with householders.'

I held my breath, wondering what Babaji would say. He laughed and gave His assent.

I brought water from the waterfall, lit the stove and placed the vessel on it. Surya Devi Baba came and sat beside me with tea leaves, milk and sugar. He again remarked, 'Vijay, in thirteen years, you're the second person from whom I'll be accepting something to drink.'

I knew that the shared tea was going to be a special moment for both of us.

When the brew was ready, I poured it into two glasses. We sat behind the hut and fell into conversation while sipping our tea. Surya Devi Baba told me the story of his life. 'Vijay, I've been serving this Goddess for thirteen years. The forest here is thick. About seven kilometres from here is a path that goes to Tanakpur. The saints say that if one meditates in Uttarakhand, or in any great place of pilgrimage, for fourteen consecutive years, then the person becomes siddha (enlightened). I have not been to the basti (settlement) for the last thirteen years, although people often come here to visit the Goddess.'

He told me that there was only a short time left for him to complete his fourteen years of sadhana. That's when I asked him something that had been niggling my mind. How had he met Haidakhan Baba a year ago, when Babaji had only appeared before the world a few months back?

Their previous encounter made for quite a gripping tale. Surya Devi Baba had fallen sick and was prey to an endless bout of vomiting, diarrhoea and fever. 'This, then, is my test,' he thought.

He vaguely remembered some Forest Department officials and contractors trying to convince him to go with them to Haldwani or Lucknow for treatment. 'But I refused,' he said. 'I told them quite clearly that I would not go anywhere. I vowed that I would live and die at the feet of the Devi.'

His well-wishers yielded before his persistence, and Surya Devi Baba kept groaning and praying to the Goddess for protection. The following morning, Lord Haidakhan arrived draped in an *andi*, which He took off and wrapped around the ailing sadhu's body.

'He came to me with a bag of reetha (soap nut) in His hand and said, "Don't worry. We are here now." He took on the role of a mother. I would vomit on Him and He would clean me up without flinching. He took complete charge of me. My smallest needs were fulfilled. I gradually started recovering.'

Surya Baba told me he believed that even his mother could not have taken better care of him, had she been there. 'His affection for me was like Ma Jagdamba's love. A week later, once I was on my feet again and could go to the temple to worship the Goddess, He told me He had to leave. He said, "We are going now. We'll come again sometime." He gave me his *andi* and said, "if you ever feel sick, cover your body with this." I saw my Eeja going away, He became invisible right before my eyes and vanished.'

The sadhu's tale made me feel blessed. I knew that it was my great good fortune that I had had the honour of making tea for him with my own hands. I also understood that Surya Devi Baba had an infinite kindness for me. At precisely that moment, Babaji called out to us. We swiftly headed into the hut. Babaji asked us if we had finished our tea. We giggled and told Him we had. He said, 'It is fine here, but do not drink tea with any householders.'

Surya Devi Baba then offered Babaji some milk and dry fruits. 'Eeja, I have told Vijay about your grandeur.'

Babaji did not comment. After a while, He told me to get some rest. It was around ten at night. Babaji then casually remarked that tigers too came from the forest for the Devi's darshan.

I got up at four in the morning. Babaji was in meditation. I went to the waterfall for my morning ablutions. By the time I returned, His meditation was over. I took out His clothes and returned to the waterfall with Him. After bathing, Babaji applied *chandan* on all of us at the hut. Gentle rays of the sun had started entering into its interiors, sparkling like gold dust. Babaji said, 'Let us take you to the Devi.'

I picked up some fruits, flowers, incense sticks and sweets and walked with Him towards the waterfall. Govardhanji and Surya Devi Baba accompanied us.

The statue of the Goddess, Surya Devi, resided in these mountains in her natural state. The branch of a peepal tree served as stairs to reach Her. These too were natural. Babaji went first. He climbed the stairs to the cave where the idol of the Goddess stood and bowed before Her. After some time, He came down and I went up with Surya Baba. There was a beauty about the place which is impossible to describe. We offered our prayers, and Surya Devi Baba helped me perform Her *aarti*. He also told me all about Her *leela*. After all the rituals were complete, we started walking back to the hut. We ambled through the forest contentedly. Surya Devi Baba was deep in conversation with Babaji, and occasionally He would smile a little.

Two days later, we were back at Haidakhan and I had stopped drinking tea—unless it was offered to me by a sadhu.

35

A MEETING OF TWO SAINTS

At this point, I would like to tell you about the meeting of two saints. As mentioned earlier, at that time there were three great saints in Uttarakhand—Babaji of Haidakhan, Nantin Maharaj, and Neem Karoli Baba. Neem Karoli Baba was a worshipper of Hanumanji. Devotees say that he had the blessings of Lord Hanuman. His ashram is in Kainchi Dham, on the way to Ranikhet from Bhimtal. He has other ashrams at Ranikhet and Vrindavan.

The second saint, Nantin Baba, was over ninety years old. In the mountains, Nantin means child. Nantin Baba was childlike in his habits and short in stature. He was a wandering saint who performed his *leela* all over Uttarakhand. His devotees lived mainly on fruits, while some survived solely on milk.

Some of Nantin Baba's devotees visited Lord Haidakhan quite often, wondering if He was really an avatar of the previous Haidakhanwale Baba. Queries put to Nantin Baba only produced a laugh. He studiously avoided a direct answer. In the meanwhile, one group of devotees was trying its best to make these two holy men meet.

In 1972, the two saints finally met at Surya Devi Baba's abode. The meeting came about through Amar Singh Yadav, a very big timber contractor in Haldwani, who originally hailed from Rajasthan. The forest where Surya Devi's cave-temple stood also came under his purview. This was where he met Babaji for the first time and fell under His spell. Gradually, his whole family became exclusive devotees of Babaji.

The meeting of the two saints had been arranged at Surya Devi's temple. Nantin Baba was already at the spot when Babaji arrived at about five in the evening from Haidakhan. A large number of devotees had accompanied Lord Haidakhan.

Nantin Baba was sitting with his devotees on one side of the pathway. As soon as Babaji passed him by, he threw flowers in His path without looking at Him. Babaji asked me to pick the flowers up. I picked them up and we walked on. A large number of followers of both Babas were present, and they were all wondering who would go to whom.

Babaji headed for His bath and then sat in meditation in the hut above. Journalists kept approaching both the Babas and repeatedly asked the same question. 'Will you to go to Him, or will He come to you?' The two saints just smiled without responding.

The night progressed, and devotees were getting worried. The whole forest had come alive with chants of '*Om Namah Shivay*'.

Amar Singhji had pitched tents for devotees to stay in the forest. At around nine that night, Nantin Maharaj called the journalist Padmaduttji and said, 'Where is Babaji staying? Take me for His darshan.'

He took out Rs 5 from his overcoat (his attire of choice in the summers) and put it on a thali with five fruits, some flowers and dry fruits. He then held Pantji's hand and walked over to Babaji's hut. Devotees of both Babas broke out in cheers, raising slogans like '*Bhole Babaji ki jai*' and '*Nantin Maharaj ki jai*'.

A group of journalists and devotees had gathered near Surya Devi Baba's hut. A fire was burning brightly in the *dhuni*, and Babaji had just asked me to place an *aasan* on His right, when Nantin Baba entered. He was less than five feet in height. He went up to Babaji and placed the *thali* (salver) at His feet and bowed to Him.

Without speaking, Babaji signalled at him to sit on the *aasan* that had been placed for him. He was seated to the right of Babaji and to the left of Surya Devi Baba. The flames in the *dhuni* were bright and warm when the three great men sat in meditation. Chants of '*Om Namah Shivay*' began. Devotees watched the scene from the sidelines with interest. I was sitting nearby looking at Babaji, who was in His meditative posture. Nantin Baba also had his head bowed as he sat in dhyan. They all meditated for about an hour. Then Nantin Baba got up, bowed to Babaji and walked towards his own accommodation.

Under orders from Babaji, I escorted him. The curiosity among devotees was palpable. They had been wondering if there would be any exchange of conversation between the two saints. None had taken place. Some journalists and devotees approached Nantin Baba. An old lady asked him what he thought of Lord Haidakhan.

He smiled and said, 'I thought He looked very old.'

The old lady looked perplexed and remarked, 'Maharaj, you look old, He is very young.'

Nantin Baba replied, 'No, He is very old.'

The old woman fell silent at Nantin Baba's reply. The editors of the newspapers *Sandesh Sagar* and *Uttarayana Weekly* tried to probe Nantin Maharaj further about Babaji, and pat came the reply: 'Babaji is a form of Lord Shiva. He will be around for some time and then He will go away. He has descended on earth for the welfare of the world, and the powers of Brahma, Vishnu and Mahesh, all reside in Him.'

This incident was published in the newspapers of the time.

Nantin Baba used to wear a loin cloth in winter and an overcoat in summer. He would also warm himself near a *dhuni* in that season.

He used to put fruits that were given to him in running water. After he met Babaji at Surya Devi, he directed his devotees to seek shelter under Lord Haidakhan.

This incident took place eight months after our first visit to Surya Devi and is an important sequel to our trip there.

After staying there for two days, we walked back to Haidakhan Dham. Surya Devi Baba's eyes were wet when the time to part with Babaji arrived.

36

A WALK TO ADI KAILASH

No one in Haidakhan slacked. The tiniest of tasks was performed with alacrity, because Babaji constantly told us that karma was a form of divine worship. He had no time for idleness and would go to great lengths to drive it away. 'The devotion of people who perform their karma evolves automatically,' He would say.

One day He announced, 'We will go to Adi Kailash tomorrow.' Around eight months had elapsed since our visit to Surya Devi. He looked at His devotees, almost as if He was asking if there was anyone among us who was unwilling to go. Everyone was willing. How could anyone miss the chance to go to Adi Kailash with Lord Shiva in the flesh?

Pantji of the forest department was sitting nearby. He was one-legged and used to walk with a crutch. He said, 'I would also like to go.'

Babaji consented.

At seven the following morning, we started out for Adi Kailash with Babaji. The mountain stood about five kilometres from Haidakhan and was a straight, steep climb. Babaji stopped at one spot and broke a leaf from a tree. He gave it to me and said, 'Birju, you will not feel thirsty.'

The joy of walking with God is like nothing else in the world. I thought of Surya Devi Baba, who had told me that a person attains siddhi after meditating for fourteen years in Uttarakhand. Anxious to satisfy my curiosity, I questioned Babaji and asked Him why this was so. He waved His hand in an arc and said, 'After meditating here for fourteen years, a man becomes enlightened.' He laughed and said, 'Birju, we have also come here for fourteen years.'

I couldn't fathom what He meant at the time. How ignorant I was! He told me so many times, 'We will do our work and leave soon.' Yet it made no impact on me. I never quite understood that He would only be with us for a short period of time.

We reached Adi Kailash. A platform had been built on a flat plateau. Two wooden poles with hundreds of bells tied to them stood there. A lot of people came here on Mondays from various parts of the mountains in Kumaon. Having heard the news of Babaji's arrival, a number of locals were already there with fruits, curd and milk. Babaji distributed it to everyone. An hour later, He announced that it was time to go back.

It is said that if a person stops at the Adi Kailash in the winter even for a day, his skin tone changes. Babaji had performed austerities on this mountain for forty-five days after He had emerged from the cave at Haidakhan.

We started our descent. I felt a little sad as we left. It was such a tranquil place, with a strange kind of purity about it.

To my immense surprise, even Pantji had reached the top chanting Babaji's name. The pride of achievement was apparent on his face. He was very happy. Prabhu had empowered all of us. Not a single devotee was tired.

37

A FRIGHT AT NIGHT

Dr Bindu and Durga Devi arrived at Haidakhan to invite Babaji to Almora. They told Him that His devotees there were eager to meet Him. Work on the boundary wall at Haidakhan was almost complete, so Babaji accepted their invitation. Our date of departure was set for 15 December.

Dr Bindu had promised to send a car to Kathgodam to fetch us. There were two of us accompanying Babaji on the trip. In those days, there was no direct road to Almora from Haidakhan. One had to walk all the way to Vijaypur (in Haldwani) and then travel onwards. We arrived at Kathgodam at about three in the morning and got into the car that was waiting for us.

We reached Almora at eight that night. All the prominent dignitaries of the town were present at Dr Bindu's house. Himself an eminent doctor in the area, all sorts of officers, lawyers, jurists and doctors were part of his social circle. Yet, at heart, he was a simple soul.

We entered a hall and Babaji was escorted to a seat that looked like a throne. Devotees queued up for His darshan. In the meanwhile, Dr Bindu's sister showed us the room that had been prepared for His

stay. She also asked us what they should serve for His *bhog*. After the darshan, devotees gradually started trickling out of the hall, and at last Babaji retreated with me to His room. Before heading there, He informed our hosts that He would apply *chandan* on everyone at four in the morning.

At around nine that evening, Dr Bindu and his sister came into the room with milk and fruits for Babaji, who was charmed by their hospitality. Dr Bindu asked Babaji if he could press His feet. Babaji acquiesced.

While Dr Bindu was pressing His feet, Babaji remarked, 'Doctor sahib, you were also our devotee in your past life.' Babaji's words evoked strong emotions in the good doctor, and his eyes filled up with tears. He continued to chat with Babaji, blissfully unaware that He had fallen asleep.

After a while, when there was no response from Babaji, it dawned on everybody present that He was fast asleep. I told Dr Bindu to get some rest and latched the door after he left. When I returned to Babaji's bedside, I noticed that He had not even drunk His milk. I tried to wake Him, but He did not respond. I made an attempt to lift Him by holding His hand, but His body was limp and fell back on the bed every time I tried to raise it.

It was soon apparent to me that He wasn't even present in His body. It was my first encounter with astral travel—the state when the soul leaves the body for a while to travel elsewhere. My first reaction was fear, but eventually I managed to work out that Babaji was off on an astral jaunt that was beyond mere mortals like me. Having satisfied myself that nothing untoward was up, I covered His body with His *andi* and lay down at His feet. I somehow fell asleep in that position.

At around four in the morning, Babaji shook my head. My eyes flew open and I saw Him sitting in a meditative position. I had my bath and then filled a bucket of water for Him in the bathroom. That

done, I became busy preparing *chandan*. After His ablutions, Babaji applied the paste on everyone and then sat in meditation again.

A large number of devotees had collected outside and preparations for the havan were underway. At around 8 a.m., I went to Babaji with some milk. It was only while He was drinking it that I remembered the previous night's incident. Beset by a strong sense of curiosity, I asked, 'Babaji, last night when I tried to wake you up to give you milk, your body was limp and kept falling again and again.'

He did not give me a direct answer. He just said, 'Never touch my body at night.'

I apologized with folded hands and promised never to do it again. It is my belief that Babaji used to visit the 'world' at night.

After the visit, we came back to Haidakhan Dham. Many foreign devotees had met Babaji at Almora and some of them now came to Haidakhan Vishwa Mahadham for darshan; chief among them was Gaura Devi.

Baba was to go to Vrindavan in the month of January. The Prakatya Utsav (festival celebrating the Appearance of Lord Haidakhan) is celebrated there in February. After the boundary wall was complete, He ordered the construction of some stairs. Then one day, He asked, 'Birju, how much money do you have?'

I said, 'Maharaj, twenty-five thousand.'

'Open a bank account in Haldwani,' He instructed.

I hesitantly refused. 'Babaji, I won't be able to do this.'

He did not persist. Instead, He said, 'Okay, then tell us the names of our devotees in Haldwani in whose name the money can be deposited.'

I gave Him the following names: 'Amar Singh Yadav, Ramprakash Bhasin, Ramesh Bhatt, Hemchand Bhatt (an advocate), Matadin Gupta and Trilok Singh.' As soon as I mentioned the last name, Babaji perked up and said, 'This one is fine. When we go to

Vrindavan, give twenty thousand to Trilok Singhji and ask him to deliver it to us at Mathura.'

Babaji was very wise. He instinctively knew whom to trust. When we reached Haldwani, en route to Vrindavan, we first stopped at Trilokji's house. The train to Vrindavan was to depart from Haldwani at five in the evening. I gave Trilokji Rs 20,000 and told him that Babaji had asked him to bring the money with him when he came to Vrindavan.

38

THE MYSTERY OF THE TULSI GARLAND

I could not understand why Babaji did not want to carry the money with Him to Vrindavan. Why did He want it delivered there instead?

All His followers in Haldwani had come to the station to see Babaji off. He and I boarded the first-class compartment, and the others who were travelling with us to Vrindavan hopped into different coaches. Standing at the door of the carriage, Babaji waved farewell to His devotees. The train reached Mathura at five in the morning.

The station was swarming with local devotees waiting to pick up Babaji. Half an hour later, we entered the temple to a tumultuous welcome; people from various places were already assembled there. After taking a bath, Babaji applied *chandan* on all of them.

During our stay at the Vrindavan temple, several peculiar incidents took place, strengthening people's belief that Babaji was Lord Haidakhan's avatar. I also had a run-in with the temple priest.

I was in charge of Babaji's *bhog*, which consisted primarily of milk, fruits and the occasional nuts. The temple priest, Hiralal Sharma, used to prepare the offerings for the idol. He was proud of being a

Brahmin, while Babaji respected people of all castes and always said that a person must be recognized by karma and not caste. I belonged to the Vaishya community, while Brahmins traditionally considered all services to God as part of their exclusive domain. Hiralal Sharma did not much care for me. Part of his grouse was that I was serving lord Haidakhan.

One day, I accidentally touched him while I was taking milk for Babaji. The priest shrieked so loudly that everyone in the temple heard him. Babaji, who was sitting with an Air Force officer at the time, came to investigate and admonished the priest when He discovered the cause. 'People come here to us for peace. If they encounter this kind of strife, why will they seek us out?'

Matters did not end here. Babaji later lectured him on the reality of human existence and punctured his false air of superiority. 'You serve Haidakhan's idol, he serves the living Haidakhan, who do you think is senior?'

Hiralal naturally had no answer and returned from the encounter a chastened man. Quite cowed by his interaction with Babaji, he actually came to me and apologized. Prabhu's message was clear: He was the Living God!

One afternoon, at around 2 p.m., not long after my skirmish with Hiralal, someone knocked at the temple door. Babaji was resting in His room. A devotee went to investigate the identity of the caller. The visitor asked for me. When I went to the door, I saw an old man in a patchwork kurta made of at least fifty pieces of cloth, standing outside with a bag slung on one shoulder.

When he saw me, he asked, 'Are you Vijay?'

I answered in the affirmative.

The old man said, 'I know you. Do you recognize me?'

I could not place the old man. I knew most of Babaji's devotees, as I had been living in close proximity with Him for a while now. But this man was a stranger.

'Everyone knows me, because I stay with Babaji,' I responded with a touch of arrogance and asked him who he was.

He smiled and said, 'That's not true. Anyway, I have come all the way from Gangotri to meet Babaji, and I am known as Gangotri Baba.'

Accepting him at his word, I ushered him in and offered him a seat on an *aasan*. 'Babaji is resting,' I informed him.

He sat on the *aasan* and then stated, 'You don't know me, Vijay, but let me tell you that in your past life, you and I served the old Baba Haidakhan together. I wonder why you have been born here.'

I was beginning to think that he was slightly mad. At the same time, something about his persona scared me. When Babaji came out of His room, I said, 'Maharaj, this is Gangotri Baba. He has come to meet you all the way from Gangotri.'

Gangotri Baba rose and fell at His feet. Babaji asked him to sit and directed me to arrange some food and water for the visitor. After he had eaten, Babaji asked, 'How are you?'

The Baba from Gangotri replied, 'I live in Jhala village near Gangotri Dham. I have come here for your darshan.'

'We gave you a garland made of Tulsi (holy basil) the last time we met, where is it?' Asked Babaji.

Gangotri Baba took out a dilapidated-looking Tulsi garland that looked very much the worse for wear and presented it to Babaji. He took it and then ordered me to arrange for Gangotri Baba's stay at a nearby dharamshala. Once his accommodation had been arranged, Babaji asked him to proceed there to rest and went back to His room.

After our guest left, Babaji called me and asked me to re-thread the garland on the morrow. I nodded and came out, my thoughts returning to Gangotri Baba. Something didn't quite add up. I kept wondering why Babaji had asked him to return the garland. It was literally falling apart.

When Gangotri Baba came to the temple the following morning, Babaji was meditating. I offered him a seat and brought some milk for him. Gangotri Baba asked me to sit beside him and proceeded to solve the mystery that had been baffling me since the previous day. He told me he had met Babaji in Haridwar, where he had been given the Tulsi garland with the instruction that he was to return it to Babaji whenever next they met again. After that, Babaji had vanished.

'I have been searching for Him ever since. I looked for Him everywhere, and then finally went to Jhala where I began my austerities. I built a hut in the village, and have been there ever since. Recently, Baba appeared to me in a vision and said, "We have reincarnated and will meet you in Vrindavan." So, I came here in search of Him. Now that I have seen Him, my life is blessed.'

His story fascinated me, and my expression must have revealed this. Suddenly Gangotri Baba said, 'Vijay, I wonder how you ended up serving Babaji. I want to go to your house and see your horoscope.'

I looked at him in alarm and tried to dissuade him. 'Baba,' I said respectfully, 'everything is fine, I don't want to know anything about myself.'

Just then, Babaji emerged from His room and came to Gangotri Baba. Devotees made a beeline for both of them. Babaji called him a great saint of this era and said that his strange clothes and that kurta made of patches of cloth reflected his simplicity. 'He's trying to hide himself from this world.'

Three days later, Gangotri Baba asked Babaji to allow him to return to Jhala. Babaji gave His consent and bade him a final farewell. I paid obeisance to the sadhu from Gangotri by prostrating at his feet. He blessed me affectionately.

I went outside to see him off, feeling quite woebegone. He got into the car that was waiting to take him away and disappeared from my life.

39

PRAKATYA UTSAV AT VRINDAVAN

One day Babaji asked me, 'Do you want to take your exams?'

I had already filled up the registration form to take my class tenth examinations privately. They were to be held in March. I said, 'Yes, Prabhu, I do.'

Babaji said, 'We will make you a scholar without studying.'

I kept quiet. Babaji was in residence at Vrindavan at that time. He intended to stay on even after the Prakatya Utsav.

In March, I went to Bharatpur to take my exams and sailed through without too much effort, thanks to Babaji's blessings. However, as always, when I went home, my mother broke down and I too became emotional. But God knows, there was a definite power that was turning me into a *nirmohi* (a person with no attachments). When I returned to Vrindavan, Baba asked me how I had done in my examinations. I told Him that I had done fine. He predicted that I would be successful.

'Prabhu, it is all due to the infinite kindness that you shower on an insignificant person like me,' I responded humbly.

In his lifetime, Mahendra Maharaj used to celebrate Babaji's Prakatya Utsav (Festival of His Appearance) with great pomp. Babaji saw no reason to discontinue the tradition. Trilok Singh had reached Vrindavan to participate in the festivities. Arrangements had been made for him to stay in the room upstairs at the Vrindavan temple.

As soon as I returned to Vrindavan after my examinations, Trilok Singhji called me. He handed over the Rs 20,000 that I had given to him in Haldwani at Babaji's request. He had tied the money to his belt and had been carrying it around on his person. I apprised Babaji of the latest development and told Him that Trilokji had returned the money to me.

'The man is honest, he is worthy of being trusted,' pronounced Babaji. By now, He had started speaking very softly.

Trilok Singh, Amar Singhji, Ramesh Bhatt, Gusain Raja, Rajendra Adhikari had all come to the temple to pay their respects to Babaji. On the day of the Prakatya festival, He was anointed with milk, and 1.25 lakh diyas were lit for the puja.

Prominent devotees of Mahendra Baba at Vrindavan, such as Chetramji, Lakshminarayanji, Ram Gopalji, Girja Shankarji, Shraddhanandji, Phoolchand Tiwari, Vaidya Nathi Lalji, Shyam Bihari Gaur, Chand Bihari Gupta, Nanak Chand Gupta, Chakleshwar Parasad, Makkhanji, Shivcharan Lal Gupta, were enrapturing everyone with their bhajans and had organized the entire affair. They also accorded Shri Trilok Singh, and all the devotees who had come from Haldwani, great respect.

Babaji's *tripund* (the three horizonal lines drawn on the forehead with *chandan*) had become a talking point in Vrindavan. Devotees would emerge from the temple sporting the *tripund*. The whole town was talking about Babaji. Acharya Vishnudutt Shastri had started giving discourses on Babaji, and his eloquence was gradually removing all doubts about Babaji's identity as Lord Haidakhan.

After the festival ended, devotees went back home. Shortly afterwards, Babaji decided to go to Jaipur, where a Srimad Devi Bhagwatam Katha and yagna was being organized in Shastri Nagar, at Mohan Lal Vaidya's house. He was also a disciple of Mahendra Maharaj.

We headed to Jaipur by car and stopped over at at my elder brother's house in Bharatpur for an hour before proceeding on our way. We reached Shastri Nagar at around 3 p.m. and were accorded a grand reception. Shri Vishnudutt Shastri had also come with us. All the arrangements for the katha and yagna were to be carried out under his supervision.

In the evenings, Shastriji would hold discourses on Babaji for devotees. Babaji would also sit through them with a smile on his face. Devotees had started pouring into Mohanlalji's house from several places for Babaji's darshan. Each morning, after the yagna, Babaji would grace the houses of various devotees with his presence. Outstation devotees were given food as prasad.

Ramkumar Sharma, a correspondent of *Lok Sena Sandesh*, had a house behind Ganganagar Hotel, which was situated in front of the Polo Victory Cinema. Babaji went there at his invitation. He had decked the entire house from top to bottom with flowers, and the aroma of incense wafted towards us from every direction. It was the same story everywhere. Old devotees were flooding in and bringing with them a vast deluge of new followers.

40

STRANGE ENCOUNTERS OF THE BLACK MAGIC KIND

Under strict instructions from Shastriji, I was standing next to Prabhu and systematically collecting various offerings—garlands, prasad and suchlike—that were being presented to Him by the vast line of devotees who had queued up for darshan.

Acharya Vishnudutt had taken me aside earlier and primed me. 'Son, you are the one who stands near Babaji. Make sure you collect the offerings directly from devotees. I have a feeling that someone will try some tantra here.'

Shastriji was a very learned man. He once told me that he had mastered the Kaal Bhairav siddhi (material, paranormal, supernatural, or otherwise magical powers, abilities, and attainments that are the products of yogic advancement through sadhana/disciplined and dedicated practice or learning especially in religion or music such as meditation and yoga). There's very little I can tell you about his scholarly knowledge. But this I can and will say, it was my privilege to have been blessed with the opportunity to be with Him at close quarters. Babaji often told Shastriji, 'Birju is your foremost disciple.'

Shastriji had a lot of affection for me and loved me like a child. He and I went everywhere with Babaji. When I did not sleep at Babaji's feet, I would share a room with him.

Mindful of his instructions, I was on full alert and meticulously started removing all the offerings from Babaji's vicinity. I noticed that Shastriji too was keeping a close watch on everyone who was approaching Babaji for His blessings.

It was around 4 p.m. and Babaji was about to go back to Shastri Nagar, when a beautiful young girl came towards Him. She had some cotton wool wrapped around a stick, which was emanating the sweet smell of *attar* (perfume). She was about to present it to Babaji when Acharyaji gestured silently, indicating that he wanted me to take it from the girl's hand. I did as I was bid, and as soon as I took possession of it, my entire hand started tingling. Shastriji immediately snatched it from me and chanted a mantra; it sparked and he threw it out of the window.

We returned to Shastri Nagar.

No further mention was made of the matter until much later. Acharyaji and I were preparing to retire for the night (we were sharing a room close to Babaji's chamber) when he broached the topic. 'Birju, there is a black magician, Moorkhanand tantric, in the hills of Galtaji. This is what I believe. He is the one who has sent the girl here to engage in *vashikaran* (hypnosis). If the girl comes back tomorrow, you must tell her without flinching that we know where she has come from and that she will not be able to practice her black magic here. Remember this, and stick to Babaji like glue.'

I pondered over what he had told me, and I am not sure when I finally fell asleep, but my eyes opened at three in the morning. After washing up, I prepared a bath for Babaji and then set out to finish my morning chores.

On the fourth day of the yagna at Vaidyaji's house, Babaji was to go to Maheshwariji's residence after the morning yagna was over.

Maheshwariji was the Director of Industries in the Government of Rajasthan, and his house was located behind the Government Hostel. He had arranged an impressive reception for Babaji.

After the kirtan, once prasad began to be distributed, Babaji went to His room to rest. I stood outside it to make sure that no one disturbed Him and fell into conversation with some devotees. Suddenly, the girl appeared and started loitering near Babaji's room. I asked her, 'What's the matter?'

She made no reply. I told her to sit outside and wait. 'Babaji is resting at the moment.'

She became angry. 'My name is Draupadi. Why did you take away the *attar* from my hand? I wanted to give it to Babaji.'

I thought it was a good time to let her know that we were onto her and said, 'I take whatever Babaji is offered. I also know that you have come from Moorkhanand, the black magician. I hope you understand that you will not be able to use your black magic here.'

My words made her furious and she threatened me. 'If you know that I have been sent by Moorkhanand tantric, you should beware.'

I was unimpressed. 'I too have a *samarth* (capable, competent and powerful) guru. You won't even be able to touch a hair of mine.'

She looked at me with great loathing and saying, 'I will not let you get out of Jaipur alive,' left the house in a fine fury.

Despite my initial bravado, I was petrified, and my terror kept growing as the hours ticked by. We left for Shastri Nagar at around 5 p.m. but I was barely registering my surroundings by then. I kept pondering over my probable fate. I was still in a haze when I gave Babaji His milk at around 9 p.m. I bowed mechanically and returned to my own room. By now the fear was like a living beast in my head.

Shastriji was still partaking of his prasad when I entered, and he offered me some.

'I don't feel like eating,' I told him.

He looked up and noticed that I was upset.

'What's the matter?' He asked.

I told him about my encounter with Draupadi.

'Don't worry,' he said, once I'd brought him up to date. 'You too have a *samarth* guru. Moorkhanand can try and do his worst. He won't succeed.'

After prasad, Shastriji lay down on his bed and I on the floor. We were both trying to sleep when I suddenly felt as if someone was pulling me. I cried out in fear and told Shastriji, 'Someone is pulling me.'

He sat up and said, 'Don't worry, nothing will happen to you.'

He caught my hand and started chanting some mantras. Tears rolled out of my eyes, and I trembled in terror. The only thing that registered in my mind was the word '*svaha*' (a sanskrit term meaning hail used at the end of a mantra in Hinduism and Buddhism) that he uttered every now and then. He did not let go of me and patiently kept up the chanting. This carried on till about midnight. He then concentrated on Bhairav and uttered some mantra before turning towards the eastern direction. I heard him utter the word '*svaha*' loudly and then he relaxed his grip on my hand.

After that, Shastriji patted my head and said, 'You have nothing to worry about anymore, son. Everything is fine now. Moorkhanand was trying to wage war on you from the hills of Galtaji through mantras. He has failed. He tried very hard but his black magic did not work. Nothing will happen to you now.'

I was too messed up to really understand what had happened to me. But I was sure of one thing. There was no way I was going to sleep on my own. Shastriji allowed me to creep up next to him on his bed. My fear gradually receded, and he watched over me until I slept. When I woke up in the morning, I put the night's events behind me and went about my everyday chores.

Later that morning, my mother's brother, Chand Bihariji, suddenly appeared, in a state of acute panic. 'Vijay, Jiji (elder sister)

Iahendra Maharaj, who had predicted the reincarnation of Haidakhan Baba before
ıking samadhi in 1969.

Haidakhan Baba, after his reincarnation, in the early 1970s.

Performing yagna with Babaji, circa 1972.

Visiting Ambalal Inamdar's school in Bombay with Acharya Vishnudutt Shastri and Babaji in 1972.

At the feet of the living God. With Babaji near His cave at Haidakhan, circa 1973.

With actor Shammi Kapoor, his wife Neila Devi and Maha Muniraj at Vrindavan Temple.

Babaji at the Mahashakti Dhuni (sacred fire). Legend has it that this sacred fire has been at Haidakhan since time immemorial. Babaji used to say, '*Guru ke bina gyan nahi, Dhuni ke bina dhyan nahi*'.

Haidakhan Baba with Rajesh Pilot, his wife, Rama, and children, Sachin and Sarika, at Haidakhan Ashram in 1981.

Actress Priyanka Chopra at Haidakhan Ashram with Dr Arvind Lal and me.

Presenting my book, *Divyanubhuti*, to Rajasthan Chief Minister Ashok Gehlot in 2021.

With my family. (L-R) My daughter, Kanika, my wife Neeru, my son, Ankit, an my daughter-in-law, Aart

is very ill,' he said, referring to my mother. 'You must go to Bharatpur right now if you want to see her for the last time.' My elder brother, Shivcharan, had relayed the news to him on the railway phone. For a moment, I was rattled, and then I calmed down.

My first thought was, how can I leave Babaji alone? It was soon obvious to me that I could not. 'I cannot leave Babaji,' I told him firmly, my mind made up. 'Tell *bhaiya* (brother).'

Mamaji was one of Babaji's most devoted disciples. He understood my response and did not admonish me. 'You have made the right decision. I will tell Shivcharan that you cannot come right now.' He left a short while later.

Perhaps God is testing me, I thought, as I took the *chandan* to Babaji's room. Shastriji was also with me. We both bowed to Him. He first applied *chandan* on Shastriji's forehead and then turned to me. 'Son, you look very dull today, what's the matter?' He asked gently as He put the paste on my brow.

I shook my head and said, 'Everything is fine.'

He gave me a penetrating stare and said, 'No, something is wrong.'

I told Him that I had received news from home that my mother was very ill and wanted to see me for the last time. But I had refused to go.

Babaji said, 'Nothing will happen to your mother. Anything else?'

I shook my head.

Shastriji then gave me a nudge and said, 'Why aren't you telling Babaji about the other matter? He is an *antaryami* (omniscient one). It's not right to hide anything from Him.'

I yielded and dutifully told Babaji about Draupadi and her attempts at *vashikaran*. I kept nothing back and also recounted the terror I had endured the night before.

Babaji smiled and said, 'We were not looking when she gave the perfume, otherwise we could have destroyed her then and there. But we cannot violate the ideals of decorum. Son, there is nothing in the world that the girl can do to us. You don't know whom you live with. *Om Shanti, Om Shanti, Om Shanti*. You have had a bad time. Go and rest.'

Shastriji and I bowed to Him and returned to our own room. Shastri began the recitation of the *Durga Saptshati*. Baba was in meditation. Later that morning, I was heating some milk for Him in one corner of the room when I heard someone knock at the door.

I opened the door and saw Draupadi standing there with fruits and flowers. I immediately slammed it shut.

She shouted from outside, 'Vijayji, open the door, I apologize to you.'

I replied from inside, 'Look, I have no quarrel with you. Let Babaji come out. Then you can talk.' I refused to let her in.

When I told Shastriji that she was outside, he remarked, 'Son, this is Babaji's pastime. He is entertaining Himself.'

At 8.30 a.m. Babaji came out to give darshan to His devotees; I was with Him. Draupadi was there too. She started beating her head before Babaji and cried, 'God, please forgive me.'

She wept so much that she fainted, and devotees had to pick her up and lay her on the sofa in front. Baba did not say anything. He just looked at me and smiled. I understood. There are some people in this world who just cannot see others happy. Imagine! She had tried to perform tantra on someone else's instruction. Babaji, however, would always maintain the boundaries of decorum.

At the end of the two-day yagna, Babaji was to go back to Vrindavan. Scenes of His departure always saddened me. Even the poet Raskhan has been unable to describe it. Each time, it was like witnessing Lord Krishna's departure from Mathura to Dwarka. Lord Krishna's gopis had ended their lives when He left them, Babaji's devotees would weep their hearts out at every separation.

In Vrindavan, Shivcharan bhaisahib told me that our mother had recovered. I was unsurprised. When Lord Shiva Himself had said nothing would happen to my mother, how was it possible for her not to get well?

From Vrindavan, Babaji planned to go to Ambaji (Gujarat), where a priest, Pandit Ramnivas, a disciple of Mahendra Maharaj, lived. Preparations to leave for Ambaji began. Shastriji came to Vrindavan from Rajgarh and we left in the morning.

41

BABAJI GOES TO AMBAJI

Maharaj Laxman Singh, a relative of the erstwhile ruler of Danta, had come to Vrindavan. There were two cars standing at the temple door in the morning to pick us up. Devotees had assembled to bid Babaji farewell. Shastriji and Puran Chand Pandey, both residents of Almora, were also going with us. We left for Ambaji in two vehicles.

Our first stop was Bharatpur, where my mother was also present. Babaji spotted her and asked, 'How are you feeling now?'

'Bhagwan, with your blessings, I am now fine,' she replied humbly.

After a short halt of about half an hour, we started out for Ambaji via Jaipur. We had to halt several times on the way as devotees waylaid us for Babaji's darshan.

At Ambaji, Pandit Ramnivasji had arranged our lodgings at a dharamshala and a large number of devotees had already gathered there. We stayed at Ambaji for three days. Our accommodation was beautifully decorated. There was a huge portrait of Goddess Durga in the room where Babaji had been billeted. After directing His devotees to go for prasad, He asked me to shut the door. I obeyed and went and sat near Him. He rose from His seat and gazed at the portrait of Durga. I felt as if He were talking to Her. He took the garland of flowers from His neck and placed it on the painting.

'Birju, how does the Devi look?' He asked.

'Very beautiful,' I responded.

'Keep offering her *bhog*,' He said.

I acquiesced. But the way He had gazed at the Devi before garlanding Her remained imprinted in my mind. I kept mulling over it and concluded that only a God could behave like this.

Kirtans would take place at Ambaji from morning to evening. Shastriji gave discourses. Devotees came and went. On the second day, the Maharaja of Danta, Prithviraj Singh, came for Babaji's darshan. He placed his head at Babaji's feet and requested, 'Please visit Danta as well.' He had come accompanied by Maharani Sahiba, his wife.

The Ambaji temple was situated to the east of the erstwhile Danta state. Maharaja Prithviraj Singh implored Babaji to visit the temple. Babaji noticed how emotional the Maharaja was becoming and acceded to his request. The temple was about a kilometre away from our accommodation. Shastriji and I sat with Babaji in the Maharaja's car, while the rest of the devotees left for the temple in other vehicles.

The Ambaji temple echoed with chants of '*Haidakhan Baba ki jai, Bhole Baba ki jai*'. A group of priests stood outside the temple to receive Babaji and Prithviraj Singh. Babaji entered the temple complex with the priests while everyone else, including the Maharaja, waited outside.

A short time later, we saw Babaji performing the *aarti* of Ma Amba. His *aarti* was distinctive. For five minutes, He performed the *aarti* of every part of Ma Amba. The priests were awestruck by His *leela*. He took the salver with various items of *aarti* into the sanctum sanctorum, where there was a large Sri Yantra (a mystical diagram consisting of nine interlocking triangles that surround a central point known as a bindu. These triangles represent the cosmos and the human body.

The priest warned Him that the Sri Yantra was so powerful that the *aarti* had to be carried out blindfolded. Those who did not cover their eyes turned blind. Babaji performed the *aarti* of the Sri Yantra without the benefit of a blindfold. He not only shocked the priest but also almost scared him to death.

After the *aarti*, Babaji came out of the temple. Devotees were eager for His darshan in the courtyard. The temple priest approached Him with an offering of a garland and shawl, followed by an *aarti*. 'He is truly the living God. Our life has been blessed because He has honoured us with His darshan,' said the priest to all the devotees who had gathered there.

Everyone became emotional at the priest's words. As Babaji got up from His seat to return to the dharamshala, the temple courtyard resounded with the chant '*Bhole Baba ki jai*'. The priest walked with us to Prithvi Singhji's car and saw us off. In no time at all, we were back at our temporary lodgings.

Babaji headed to His room, and Maharaja Prithviraj Singh left for Danta with fresh orders from Lord Haidakhan. Shastriji and I went into our own sleeping quarters. It was conveniently located near Babaji's bedchamber. The others were either receiving prasad or resting.

On the second day, Pandit Ram Niwas took Babaji to the Ganpatnath temple. Lord Haidakhan sat there for a while on a rock, soaking in the beauty of the place.

Some sadhus from Koteshwar came for Babaji's darshan and requested Him to make a trip to Koteshwar Dham, which was about five kilometres from Ambaji, where there was a very old Shiva temple. Babaji accepted their invitation.

We left for Koteshwar the following morning. En route, some Gujarati devotees from Ambaji took Lord Haidakhan to Kailash Tikri. It was not very far from Ambaji. Today, a temple dedicated to Haidakhan Baba stands there with a gaushala beside it. Devotees from Gujarat tend to it. It is a picturesque place with a 360-degree view of Ambaji.

A tremendous welcome awaited Babaji at Koteshwar. It was a beautiful place, quiet, serene and full of trees. It also had a small waterfall. There were two temples in the dham: a very old Shiva temple, and a Valmiki temple that was more recent in origin. The entire ashram had been adorned and festooned and its inmates were very humble.

Babaji was first seated on the verandah on an *aasan*, where the sadhu offered prayers to Him and then ushered Him into a room. Lodging had also been arranged for all the devotees who had accompanied Him. Shastriji and I had been assigned a room adjoining Babaji's, and one of its doors opened onto His chamber.

A kirtan was held, and after that everyone retired for a rest. Babaji too went into His room. Shastriji and I chatted with the sadhu from Koteshwar. After the evening *aarti* and kirtan, all the devotees took prasad and retired for the night. Babaji was to leave for Baroda the next day. Shastriji was going back to Rajgarh, where he taught at a government school.

42

FROM BARODA TO PAVGARH

Babaji and I left for Baroda in a jeep that belonged to Laxman Singhji. Our luggage had already been stowed into the vehicle. Shastriji took the Lord's leave. Ramnivasji's brothers were dropping him to the station. It was an emotional moment for him; he obviously found the parting difficult. There was a second jeep which was occupied by my brother Shivcharanji, his wife, and some devotees from Gujarat. I was with Babaji.

Laxmanji drove the jeep when we set out for Baroda. We stopped at several places, as he wanted to show Babaji the countryside. We reached Baroda at around five in the evening and halted at the residence of a local journalist who was hosting us. His flat was on the fifth floor. He performed Babaji's *aarti* and then ushered us into the room that had been prepared for Him.

Puran Chand Pandeyji and I were both in the room when Babaji made us lock it from inside after our host had left. 'We will not drink water or consume any eatables here. The two of you will also not eat here,' He announced.

We looked at Him in astonishment, wondering what had brought on this decree. However, neither of us had the courage to question

Him. We had some fruits and raw coconut with us. I diffidently requested Him to at least have what I was carrying. After much coaxing, He drank some coconut water. He looked very sad but we did not know why.

Pandeyji and I sat at His feet and ate some fruits. I saw Babaji gesticulating at a picture of Badri Vishal that was hanging in the room. He seemed to be engaged in some kind of conversation with it. I signalled to Pandeyji, who had his back towards Babaji's feet, and he smiled. Babaji took off the garland of flowers around His neck and put it on the picture. Pandeyji jokingly asked, 'Babaji, what discussions were you having with the Big Babaji?'

Babaji just laughed and as usual ducked the question.

After we'd finished eating, Babaji said, 'You can open the door now, but you are not to eat anything here.'

Outside, devotees from Baroda were eagerly waiting for His darshan. As soon as the doors opened, they started coming. The evening kirtan began and continued till eight at night.

As soon as He came back to His room, He declared, 'We will not stay here.'

This was the first time I had seen Babaji in such a tizzy. I couldn't make out why. He neither ate nor drank water that night. We were booked to leave Baroda on the Janta Express on the third day of our stay. I wondered how we would survive.

The next morning, once He was free after the morning rituals, Babaji made an announcement. 'Tell Laxman Singh we will go for a walk somewhere at 11 a.m.'

I passed on Babaji's message to Laxman Singh. He returned with two jeeps.

'Let's go. There's some lake here, take us there,' Babaji told him.

Sharmaji, a renowned journalist in Baroda, was approached for directions. He volunteered to accompany us. We got into the jeeps and set off to explore the city. Laxman Singhji drove us to the lake, and once we had reached, Babaji walked towards its waters with some devotees. He entered the lake and drank some water using lotus flowers as drinking vessels. As He walked back, He caught sight of some hills in the distance and asked Sharmaji, 'What are those?'

Sharmaji said, 'Prabhu, that is Pavgarh, a holy place which consists of many temples sacred to Jains. There is also a Kali temple there.'

'We will go there,' announced Babaji.

'Alright Prabhu, I'll make the arrangements,' said Sharmaji.

Things were set in motion. The programme was to pack up and head there with our luggage, as we were leaving for Vrindavan by train the following day. Sharmaji booked three rooms in the guest house at Pavgarh. Babaji finally accepted some refreshment once we reached our new lodgings. He sipped coconut water and announced, 'We'll go up the hill now to the Kali temple.'

Since the temple was around three kilometres away, Sharmaji was horrified and tried to dissuade Him. 'Prabhu, no one goes there at this time, as the path to the temple goes through a thick forest.' Babaji paid no heed and took off after instructing us to meet Him at the Jain temple the next morning.

It was 6.30 p.m. and Pandeyji and I looked at each other, aghast. I quickly took out Babaji's clothes and thrust them into his hands. 'Go after Him,' I urged. 'If I go, He will get angry.'

Pandeyji was happy to undertake the task. He hurried out and broke into a sprint to catch up with Babaji, while the rest of us resigned ourselves to a wait till morning, but a sense of unease hung in the air. After prasad that evening, the devotees started a kirtan. I sat with them but was prey to all kinds of imaginings and kept obsessing about Babaji's welfare.

After sometime, Sharmaji's daughter, who had been peering out from the verandah, exclaimed, 'Look! Babaji is there!'

We all rushed out and stared at the top of the hill. We saw a beam of a light shining on the mountain, moving hither and thither in a horizontal line. At that moment, we heard a thud and discovered that the girl had fainted. A short while later, she regained consciousness and started crying. All of us tried to calm her down. She was barely fourteen or fifteen years old.

I asked her what the matter was, and she answered with fear, 'I saw Babaji inside the light of the circumference of the moon. This was His *leela*.' We spent the next few minutes pacifying her. Once she had quietened down, we went inside and called it a night.

We were up at five in the morning and started climbing up the hill, chanting '*Om Namah Shivay!*' None of us had slept very well in our anxiety over Babaji and Pandeyji, and we wanted to catch up with them as quickly as possible. The Jain temples were on the way to the Kali temple. We espied a pond near the temples. Its water was milky white. Sharmaji told us that there were many ponds in the area with water that looked like milk.

We finally saw Babaji in the courtyard of the Jain temple at around eight in the morning. Pandeyji was with Him. We greeted Him rapturously. He said, 'You must all go and visit the Kali Mata temple.'

We bowed to Him and walked on to the Kali temple, while He stayed behind and awaited our return. After half a kilometre, we saw an old temple. We climbed the stairs and once we reached the top, we came upon a statue of Ma Kali. The idol was splendid. My eyes shifted and I noticed a small mosque above the temple. I asked Sharmaji about it. He told me that it had been built by some Muslim ruler. He also informed me that both a priest and a Maulvi lived there and that people of both religions visited the place. The priest looked after the temple, while the Maulvi tended to the mosque.

Our return to the Jain temple was much faster than our hike uphill, and Babaji came out as soon as we arrived. 'Time to go back,' He said.

On the way down, recalling the incident of the previous evening, some devotees told the Lord, 'You appeared to your devotees in the form of lights last night.'

He smiled but deflected the question, remarking, 'What a strange situation! A mosque has been built above the temple. Nobody has the power to remove it from here. We will build a Kali temple in Gujarat.'

Over time, He built a grand Kali temple in Manda village near Vapi in Gujarat. Even today, devotees gather there on every Shivaratri. All rituals are followed strictly when prayers are offered to the goddess. Yogendra Bhai and his wife Palluben are still in charge of looking after the temple.

Thinking over Babaji's words, I thought that He was right in wanting to build a new Kali temple. The thought of a Muslim ruler building a mosque on top of the Kali temple did not sit well with me. I was just beginning to wonder when the new temple would be built when I reached the guest house. All thoughts of temples and mosques fled, and I got busy packing up for our journey ahead.

43

BABAJI AND THE SPY

We left Baroda for Mathura by the Janata Express. Our bookings had been done and Babaji travelled—for the first and last time—in a three-tier sleeper. Sharmaji came to the station to say goodbye to Babaji. My brother Shivcharanji's family was with us. Pandeyji was going straight to Delhi, where he worked in a government department. We boarded the compartment, leaving behind some very tearful devotees at the station.

An upper and a lower berth had been reserved for Babaji. I spread out an *aasan* for Him on the upper berth, although He sat on the berth below, initially. Someone was smoking a bidi (a cheap and strong cigarette made from tobacco rolled in a betel leaf) in the compartment, a tea vendor was crying out in a sing-song voice, trying to sell his brew, and I was requesting people with folded hands to move forward. It was all very stressful. But Babaji was untouched. 'Never mind,' He said gently, and I subsided. Bhaisahib and his family occupied the front seats. Being in the railways, he was on familiar terms with the ticket collector.

After some time, a person came to Babaji and stared at Him. Suddenly he said, 'I saw you in Bombay yesterday.' Babaji was silent.

The man looked like the persistent type, so I decided to step in. I said, 'Bhaiya (brother), we have not come from Bombay. We are coming from Baroda.'

But he stuck to his guns and refused to back off. He told us he was a journalist and would broadcast Babaji's message to the nation. He disappeared for a few moments, only to return armed with a notebook and pen, and started nagging Babaji for an interview. But despite much pleading, Babaji remained mum. Routed, he returned to his seat. By now, I was wondering why Babaji was travelling in an ordinary compartment. At night, Babaji went up to the upper berth to rest and I lay down on the lower one. When I woke up, I found Him sitting in His meditative posture on the seat. We reached Bharatpur at 8.30 a.m. My brother's family deboarded, but Shivcharan bhaisahib came with us to Mathura.

We reached Mathura at 9 a.m. and the station was jampacked with devotees from Vrindavan, who were waiting to welcome Babaji. A car awaited Him outside. When we emerged from the station, Babaji's eyes fell on a sadhu. He called me and said, 'Go call that sadhu.'

I spoke to the sadhu and brought him to Babaji, who said, 'You can come with us to Vrindavan.'

He was more than willing and accepted Babaji's invitation with alacrity. He accompanied us in the car to the Vrindavan temple. Once there, Babaji flung further instructions at us as He went for His bath.

'Arrange his stay at Gopal Bhavan. *Inhe nehlao, dhulao aur khilao* (Bathe him, wash him and feed him).'

Chetramji proceeded to make the arrangements, and Lakshminarayanji took the sadhu along with a few other devotees and laid out quite a lavish feast for him. Then they told him to rest. Babaji called out to us after He was done with His daily routine and asked, 'Where is that sadhu?'

We informed Him that the sadhu was resting in Gopal Bhavan. He said, 'Go quickly and get rid of him from there. This is our order.'

Chetramji, Lakshminarayanji and I looked at Him, perplexed. Babaji, again said, 'Go! It is our order.'

The three of us walked to Gopal Bhavan, wondering what was wrong with Babaji. First He had asked us to arrange lodgings for the sadhu, and now He wanted us to chuck him out!

The sadhu was resting when we knocked on his door. We requested him to leave, but he ignored our plea. He was obviously very comfortable and in no mood to venture out into the big bad world. But when Chetramji told him severely that it was Babaji's order, he hastily got up and left. His reluctance was obvious. We locked up Gopal Bhavan and went back to the temple. Babaji was sitting on His chair. 'Has he gone?' He asked. We answered in the affirmative, and He said, 'If someone comes and asks for him, tell them that there is no one here.'

We were even more puzzled.

We received our prasad and went to rest in a room in the temple. At around 2 p.m. we heard a knock on the temple door. I got up and went to open it. There were three to four policemen outside. Chetramji and Lakshminarayanji had followed me out of curiosity and were standing behind me. We looked at the cops in surprise. One of them inquired about the sadhu and asked if he was with us. We answered in the negative, and they left.

I shut the door, and we all trooped into Babaji's room. Chetramji recounted the incident to Him. Babaji laughed and told us that the sadhu was a Pakistani spy.

'If he's a spy, why did you bring him here, and why did you do so much for him?' I asked.

As usual, He blindsided me with a smile and avoided an answer.

44

BABAJI GETS A SHAVE

Babaji was still in Vrindavan. One day, He espied some boys from Delhi at the Kirtan Hall. They were disrupting the kirtan by pressing their shoulders against anyone who came in front of them. Observing their antics, Babaji remarked to me, 'These children seem to be very upset with their folks. Why not get their mundan (tonsure ceremony) done?'

He summoned the children and apprised them of His decision. They burst into tears. In those days, the shaven look was not particularly fashionable. Babaji, unfazed, said, 'Don't worry. We are only destroying your ego.'

The parents of the children heeded Babaji's orders and set about convincing their offspring to shave their heads. The kids finally caved in and agreed to have their heads tonsured. From then on, it became customary for every child who came to the ashram to have his head shaved. I too grudgingly submitted to having my head tonsured. The upshot was that, subsequent to this episode, all Babaji's younger disciples stood out everywhere, thanks to their shaven heads and the *tripund* on their brow.

That night, Babaji explained the reasoning behind His latest decree. 'The hair is a symbol of your ego. Today, you look like you did the day you were born. Your tonsured head shows you a picture of yourself as you really are and kills your ego.'

Babaji once went to Benares (now Varanasi) with devotees who had come from various parts of the country. They stayed with Him in a big dharamshala. He ordered them all to get their heads shaved. Some complied happily, others under compulsion. That's when Harishankar Bhatt of Bandikui said, 'Babaji,' he said, 'everyone is getting their head shaved. Why don't you get yours shaved too?'

Sensitive to His devotee's wish, Babaji acceded and said, 'Pirji, no one has told us to shave our head till today, but now since you have asked us, we will do it.' (Harishankar was better known as 'Pir', a moniker that had been conferred on him by Lord Haidakhan.)

When word of Pirji's plea spread among Babaji's devotees, they were dismayed and begged Babaji to change His mind. 'You look good, just as you are,' they insisted.

Pirji was prepared to withdraw his words, but Babaji was adamant. He said, 'You obey every command of ours. Should we disregard the feelings of a devotee? It would be contrary to the principles of decorum.'

With these words, He went ahead and had His head tonsured in Benares. After the shave, His appearance grew even more childlike. God comes in all forms.

45

BABAJI'S LEELA

One day, Babaji went out in a tonga to the Madhuban temple near Mathura, with Makkhanji. This gentleman was the priest there and was very attached to Babaji. I was left behind at the Vrindavan temple with the rest of the devotees.

Evening came. The day drew to a close and Babaji did not return. I became quite anxious; He had not even taken any clothes with Him. I conveyed my distress to Amolak Chand Jain, a resident of Jaipur, and Nahar Singh Yadav, father of Capt. BN Yadav and father-in-law of Amar Singhji's daughter. The three of us decided to fetch Babaji and informed the rest of the devotees that we were going to Madhuban.

We hopped on to a tempo and set forth for Makkhanji's house at Madhuban. Dusk had set in by the time we reached his place. Babaji had apparently withdrawn into a room, while the priest and his family were strolling outside the house. Though Makkhanji was happy to see us, his surprise at our arrival was perceptible.

'Isn't Babaji returning to Vrindavan today?' We asked him.

'Not today,' he informed us. 'He's staying here tonight.'

We told him that we'd like to have Babaji's darshan. He nodded and told us to come into the house and wait at the door of His room.

We waited for darshan outside His room while Makkhanji went in to perform His *aarti* and inform Him of our arrival. After the *aarti*, we clearly overheard him telling Babaji, 'Vijay and two other people have come from Vrindavan.'

Babaji asked, 'Why have they come?'

'I have brought your clothes,' I chipped in from outside.

'Give the clothes to Makkhan,' He instructed. We prayed for His darshan.

'No darshan,' He announced. We then heard Him saying, 'Makkhan, we'll be having khichdi—do they think they'll be getting halwa-puri?'

We hastened to assure Him from the door that we would eat whatever He ate.

'Let them have khichdi for their supper,' He directed. 'And put them up in the other room. We will leave for Vrindavan tomorrow.'

We came away, defeated, and lay down in the room that had been allotted to us. It was situated near the door at the front of the house.

I was despondent. We had come to fetch Babaji, and if we had returned without Him, the other devotees would have made fun of us; and now we were stuck here for the night with Babaji, who was not only fuming and but also recalcitrant. I fell asleep, still brooding over our plight.

I got up at around 3.30 a.m. and went to wash up at a large pond outside. While I was in the water, I spotted a person stealthily making off with someone who looked like Babaji. They had covered themselves with a sheet and seemed to be heading towards Mathura. I thought my mind was playing tricks on me. Amolakji and Naharji joined me shortly afterwards, and I dismissed the incident from my mind.

I returned to the house. There was a *dhuni* and temple there, which still exists even today. As I started preparing *chandan* for Babaji, I heard Makkhanji's daughter laughing at me. I thought she was snickering at my bald head. Amolakji and Naharji had returned from their bath by then.

'Why are you laughing at me, sister?' I asked.

'Who are you preparing that *chandan* for?'She asked.

'Babaji,' I replied.

'Babaji left for Vrindavan at four in the morning,' she said.

I glared at her, unwilling to believe what I had heard. I went straight to His room. His clothes were still there. But He was gone. She was obviously correct. Babaji had gone off to Vrindavan without us! I wrapped all His garments in a blanket, feeling rather foolish.

Quite glum by now, my companions and I prepared to leave for Vrindavan. But she stopped us, saying, 'Babaji told me to send you only after serving you tea.'

Since Madhuban was only about three kilometres from Mathura, I told her, 'Okay. But make the tea quickly.'

Still marvelling over Babaji's great escape, I wondered how He'd managed His break-out from under our noses. Overcome with curiosity, I finally asked, 'We were sleeping near the door. How did Babaji leave?'

'He climbed the roof of this room and jumped off,' Makkhanji's daughter replied.

That was when I noticed that there were still some marks that bore witness to the fact that someone had climbed up the wooden stairs at the back of the room that led to the terrace.

After finishing our tea, we trundled from Madhuban to Mathura. There were very few available modes of transport in the area at that time. After a seemingly endless and depressing hike, we reached Mathura.

My elderly companions were by now getting tired, and I was quite distressed over their condition. I kept wondering why we had thought of fetching Babaji. Even more depressing was the prospect of being the butt of endless ribbing by devotees when we got back.

I could not understand why Babaji had left these two devotees in the lurch, especially when they had come down all the way from Vrindavan to fetch Him. Why had He done this? One of the two men I had spotted slinking away that morning had definitely been Babaji.

At long last, our troubles were at an end. We had reached Mathura's main road. Spotting a tempo heading in our direction, we flagged it, and to our immense relief, it stopped. Even better, the driver agreed to take us to Vrindavan. We climbed in at once, thankful to rest our feet, and asked him to hurry up and take us to the temple as fast as he could.

By the time we reached the temple, the sun was quite bright. Babaji was seated on His *aasan*. We slipped in quietly. I kept His belongings in a corner and bowed to Him. He laughed loudly. Amolakji and Naharji also sat down after bowing before Him. Funnily, all the other devotees thought that we had arrived with Babaji.

I sidled out of the room and bore down on Makkhanji, who was sitting in another room in the temple, adjacent to the hall. We often sat there because it had a fan.

'When did you arrive?' I asked him.

'Ten minutes ago,' He answered. 'We came on a tonga.'

I finally understood why the devotees had thought that we had come together.

We strolled out of the room. 'Why did you do it?' I asked Makkhanji.

'Babaji ordered me to,' he replied. 'He got up at three in the morning and said, "Makkhan, we will go to Vrindavan." I then said, "Prabhu, Vijay and the others are sleeping by the door." He said, "Take us upstairs to the terrace. We will get down from there and leave. If we go from the front, Birju will see us, so hide us with your *andi*." I saw you bathing in the pool at that time.'

'Makkhanji,' I said sadly, 'even if He had gone out of the front door, tell me, could I have stopped Him? Would I have had the courage?'

'Bhai, what can I say? He was amusing Himself. It's all Babaji's *leela*. He sometimes does and says strange things which make no sense to us. But they always have some underlying meaning and are done to teach us a lesson not always apparent to us. On the way here, He told me that this is how He will go one day. His devotees will be waiting outside His hut thinking He is inside, but when they open the door, He will not be there.'

They were prescient words which got lost in His various diversions, His unending *leela*, and we all forgot that we only had Him on loan for a short time. But I want to tell you that when He left His mortal body on 14 February 1984, He was inside a hut. All His devotees were waiting outside. It was only when one of them opened the door of Babaji's hut in the afternoon that they discovered He had left His body. It happened just as He had predicted.

In the initial years, He would often remind us, 'We have only come for some time.' But none of us paid any attention. He displayed His *leela* to Makkhanji in 1972. But we were so mesmerized by His presence that we all forgot that Babaji would leave us one day, after building several temples in the world in just a short span of fourteen years.

46

BABAJI GOES TO GWALIOR

After visiting Makkhanji, Babaji had left Vrindavan for Gwalior to perform a nine-day yagna for Lakshminarayanji and his family.

Lakshminarayanji used to live with his brothers in Gwalior. They had redecorated their house from top to bottom, because Babaji was coming. The *yagyashala* (a place where several priests sit and perform yagnas) had been built in the grounds in front of their compound. Thousands of devotees came for Babaji's darshan. Shri Vishnudutt Shastri was slated to recite the story of the Shrimad Devi Bhagwatam in Sanskrit during the day, and in the evening he would give discourses on it in Hindi. Some people in the pandal asked, 'Why doesn't Babaji deliver some sermons?'

Shastriji responded, 'I have also been making the same plea. "*Haidakhandi, Haidakhandi, Haidakhandi Sadasiva Samb Sadasiva, Samb Sadasiva Bol Palak Jagapati Bol*", meaning, I am also praying to Prabhu to give us a sermon.'

Lord Haidakhan spontaneously intervened and said, 'We will speak when the time is right.'

Later that evening, when Shastriji, Laxminaryanji and I were in Babaji's room, Shastriji asked, 'Maharaj, why don't you give sermons?'

Babaji said with a smile, 'Shastriji, we could give a sermon, but first tell us who will follow it? They will only say that this is what has been written in the Ramayana, this is what Swami Vivekananda has said, and Lord Krishna has said this as well. They will just say that we have heard all this before. That is why we make you all do the *jaap* (chanting). We want to empower you through chanting, so that if we say something in the future, you will follow it.'

The Lord's words silenced Shastriji.

On the third day of the yagna, Lakshminarayanji came to Babaji and said, 'Vijaya Raje Scindia, Rajmata (Queen Mother) of Gwalior, is coming for your darshan.'

Word had spread in Gwalior that a very big saint, whom devotees considered an incarnation of Shiva, was in town. At 11 a.m. the Rajmata came to see Babaji with her people in two cars. After bowing to Babaji, she requested Him to pay a visit to her palace for a yagna. Babaji accepted her invitation and went to the palace with some devotees after the havan the next day.

Rajmata received Him at the palace with great fanfare and placed Him on the throne. She washed the Lord's feet using gold and silver utensils; this was followed by an *aarti*. Shastriji has described this incident in the modern *Lila Sudha Kalash*, the last part of *Sadashiva Charitamrit*, on Babaji's orders.

47

IN MAYANAGRI, BOMBAY

After Gwalior, Babaji was to go to Bombay to Manhar Lal Vora's residence; he was one of Mahendra Maharajji's devotees. He had published many books on Babaji and had been pressing Him to grace his house. After the yagna in Gwalior was over, Babaji had stayed on for another day. Manhar Lal and Ambalal Inamdar flew in from Bombay to pick up Babaji by air—another first for Babaji!

Manhar Lalji bowed to Babaji and said, 'Prabhu, tomorrow morning we will be taking you to Bombay by plane.'

The schedule had already been set.

The next day, Shastriji and I went to Bombay with Babaji. The air trip was a first for all three of us. Shastriji was very nervous. Lakshminarayanji had come to the airport with some local devotees. Their eyes were damp as they saw us off.

We reached 'Mayanagri' (the city of illusions) Bombay, in practically no time at all. A large number of Swamiji's devotees who hailed from Bombay had come to the airport to receive Babaji. He was ushered into a car bedecked with flowers.

Manharji lived in Sion Circle in Bombay. We were welcomed at the door of his house by Voraji's daughter-in-law Jayashree, his son Dr Arun Vora, Inamdarji's wife Kusumji, and a few other devotees.

I was overawed by the magnificent buildings in the city and thought this was truly a city of illusions. Babaji ascended the stairs inside the house. I looked about me appreciatively. Voraji had a very beautiful home. I put Babaji's belongings in a large room. Shastriji and I were to share a room nearby. After His feet had been washed and *aarti* had been performed, some orange juice was offered to Him as *bhog*. Babaji then dismissed everyone and told us to get some rest. We all received prasad and trooped out. Devotees left for their respective homes, and Shastriji and I went to our room.

Once we were alone, Shastriji told me all about the Voras. They were the ultimate devotees of Shri Mahendra Baba and had sent many books that he (Shastriji) had written to Mahendra Maharajji in Vrindavan. They were extremely wealthy and yet very simple people who owned a movie hall at the back of the building where we were staying. It was called Rupam Cinema. In fact, they owned all the shops in the building.

After bathing in the evening, Babaji applied *chandan* on all the devotees who were present. In those days, Babaji used to apply *chandan* on His followers with both hands.

Devotees were increasing day and night. Old disciples were bringing in new ones. Mahendra Maharaj had once written a couplet on Babaji:

Ghar ghar jaye bhakt sab taare,
Kiye deen sab bhaanti sukhare.

(He went to the houses of all his devotees like a lodestar/And made everyone happy.)

Shastriji had also prophesied that 'the nature of God will be very simple', and his prediction about Babaji had turned out to be prescient. Everything that Swamiji told his devotees about Babaji proved true. He not only passed all the tests that were set for Him, but was exactly as Swamiji had said He would be—innocent, yet all-knowing!

Time flew by, and a routine set in. During the day, Babaji would visit the houses of various devotees in Bombay. People would stare at Him on the streets. Several took to following Him wherever He went. Laxman Singh came to Bombay from Danta to see Him. One day he brought his cousins to Voraji's house. Neila Devi and her brother Raghuveer Singh were also residents of Bombay.

Laxman Singh was extremely fond of me. Babaji had yet to emerge from His room. He introduced me to Neilaji and said, 'Vijay Bhai, she is my relative. Shammi Kapoor, the actor, is her husband. This is her brother, Raghuveer Singh.'

I'd been a movie buff of sorts as a child and was thrilled when I discovered that Shammiji, one of my favourite matinee idols, was Neilaji's spouse. I immediately went to Babaji's room and informed Him of their arrival. When Babaji came out, all the devotees present paid obeisance to Him.

Laxman Singhji took over the introductions and presented Neilaji. Babaji smiled and blessed her and Raghuveerji and asked me to give them some prasad.

Voraji and his family requested Babaji to grace their cinema hall, Rupam, with His presence.

Babaji laughed and said, 'We will definitely come.'

On the following day, Babaji was escorted to Rupam. The Vora family welcomed Him there with an *aarti*. Babaji was seated in the balcony and the movie began. It was the opening show of a film called *Maalik* (1972). Babaji sat in the theatre for about half an hour and then left for Voraji's house with a smile on His face. Everyone else also followed suit. How compassionate He was! He had gone to a movie just to please His devotees!

The next day, Babaji had to go to Ambalal Inamdar's school, 'Fellowship' where arrangements had been made to honour Babaji. We were ferried to the school in cars and were informed that prasad had also been arranged for devotees there. A lot of children studied in the school, which was run by his wife, Kusum.Vora Sahib was with us.

Babaji received a magnificent welcome at the school.

Kusumji was present at the main gate with her staff and some devotees, and they made Babaji stand on a beautifully-made rangoli and performed His *aarti* while singing a *mangal geet* (song sung on auspicious occasions) to welcome Him. He was then ushered into a hall and seated on an *aasan*, where His *charan puja* (worshipping of the Guru's feet) was followed by another *aarti*. Voraji's son Arun and daughter-in-law Jayashree had also come for the event.

Babaji had an acute sense of humour and often played pranks. On this occasion, He decorated Shastriji very beautifully with garlands, causing a great deal of mirth. Inamdarji's son, who was photographing the entire affair, showed one of the snaps to Babaji. Thereafter Babaji went to rest, while devotees lined up for prasad.

Just then, Jamunadas Ladiwali arrived and Inamdarji took him to Babaji. Once the introductions were over, Inamdarji said, 'Maharaj, he donated a lot of money to Mahendra Maharaj for the construction of the Vrindavan Ashram.'

Babaji immediately asked Shastriji to hand over some prasad to Ladiwaliji and invite him to the Vrindavan Ashram. At four in the evening, we went back to Voraji's house. It was now overrun with devotees eagerly waiting for Babaji's darshan. Babaji went for a bath and then applied *chandan* on everyone. Once He sat on His *aasan* in the hall, they rushed forward to meet Him. The bhajan singers Voraji had organized that evening lent a melodic backdrop to the whole scene. There was a joyous air all around as bhajans echoed throughout the building and wafted out skywards into the cosmos. Every last one of us felt as if we had become one with God.

Lord Haidakhan was distributing prasad to devotees with His own hands when Laxman Singh, Neilaji and Raghuveer Singh dropped in for another darshan. Neilaji and Raghuveerji pleaded with Babaji to pay a visit to their father's house. He told them that He would come the next day.

On the following day, Babaji visited their father Colonel Ajit Singh's residence. They all greeted Babaji and took Him to a takht inside a big room. After washing Babaji's feet, Neilaji's father performed an *aarti*, accompanied by chants of '*Om Namah Shivay*'. One by one, devotees presented garlands of flowers to Babaji. My eyes, in the meanwhile, were on a handsome man who was taking Babaji's photographs from a distance.

Raghuveerji said, 'Vijay bhai, that's my brother-in-law, Shammi Kapoor.'

What a big name he was! I thought, wonderingly.

Neilaji went with a wreath to her husband and took him to Babaji. She bent down and placed the wreath at Babaji's feet. Babaji smiled and blessed them. Shammi immediately retreated into the distance and resumed his tryst with his camera.

Babaji subsequently went to a room that had been readied for Him. Neilaji's father, brother, bhabi (brother's wife) all followed Him in to offer Him *bhog*.

Neilaji came to me and said, 'Vijay bhai, tell Prabhu he (Shammi) drinks too much.' She was obviously very worried about her husband's penchant for alcohol.

I went to Babaji and said, 'Neilaji is saying that Shammiji drinks too much liquor.'

He looked at her and said, 'Liquor is for drinking. Our Gods used to call it sura and consumed it. Men drink it and call it madira.'

His words distressed me, and I felt very bad. Neilaji had gone pale with fear.

When Babaji rose to leave the room, He said, 'Everything will be alright. Tell Neilaji not to worry.'

Neilaji feared for her husband's health, but as usual Babaji was right. In due course of time, Shammiji not only became Lord Haidakhan's follower but also quit drinking, earning the affectionate moniker 'Mahatmaji' from Babaji. He started visiting Haidakhan and Vrindavan quite frequently, and Babaji too later visited him at his house in Bombay.

He even organized Shammiji's only son Aditya's wedding in Haidakhan. The Kapoor family attended Aditya's wedding in full force, along with a number of bigwigs from the film industry that included another Bollywood icon, Raj Kapoor. The entire event was very different from the usual traditional affairs.

By the time we went back to Voraji's house that evening, Raghuveerji and Neilaji had started treating me like a brother, showering me with a great deal of affection. The following evening Raghuveerji brought two cine artistes, Chetan Anand and Priya, for Babaji's darshan; they both proceeded to offload their personal problems on Babaji. Raghuveerji later introduced them to Shastriji and me.

I had hit cloud nine by this time and was over the moon at the mere thought of all the actors I was encountering. I was also seized by an avid desire to witness a shooting. Raghuveerji was amused and shepherded me to a shoot one afternoon when Babaji had retired to His room. He took me to Chetan Anand's studio to watch the shooting of *Hindustan Ki Kasam* (1973), a Raj Kumar and Priya starrer. I was, needless to say, absolutely ecstatic. I may not have been your garden variety teenager, but I was still young enough to enjoy the experience as much as any other kid on the block.

We had been in Bombay for ten days. The Lord ordered Shastriji to make arrangements for our return to Vrindavan. We informed Voraji of our plans. He pleaded with Babaji to stay a little longer, but

Babaji said, 'No, we have already been here too long, we will come back some other time.'

Vora sahib booked tickets for everyone in the first-class compartment of the Paschim Express. Shivcharan bhaiya too had come to Bombay to escort Babaji back to Vrindavan. He had a railway pass. Babaji stood at the door of the compartment and waved. Devotees began to raise slogans in tribute to Babaji. As there was still some time for it to leave, people inside the train hopped off to watch the spectacle.

As soon as the train moved, Babaji entered the cabin and took His seat. Shastriji and I were with Him. At several stops, Shivcharanji would bring the railway staff for His darshan. We reached Bharatpur at around six in the morning, where many devotees were waiting at the platform to see Lord Haidakhan.

Babaji stood at the door of the compartment and blessed them. Half an hour later we were at Mathura, where devotees from Vrindavan had come to receive Babaji. We got into a waiting car and sped off to our destination.

48

LIGHTS FROM THE SKY

Babaji stayed in Vrindavan for a month, and devotees from various parts of the country swarmed to see him. Their numbers were increasing exponentially and people were finding it difficult to enter the temple courtyard. Later, with Babaji's permission, a temple at Gwalior was opened up to devotees, and Babaji started going there to grant them darshan.

One day, Babaji suddenly went to Mahendra Maharajji's farm at Bhainsa Village, which was located behind the Mathura Refinery. It was here that Swamiji's supreme devotee Chetramji lived with his family. Chakleshwar, who was devoted exclusively to Babaji, also resided with them. After I went home, he served Babaji for some time. Lord Haidakhan wedded him to Phoolchand Tiwariji's daughter at Madhuban. Phoolchandji, a jailer by profession, hailed from Behror, Rajasthan. Chakleshwar used to treat me like a brother. After staying at the farm for two days, Babaji returned to Vrindavan.

Shraddhanandji, a lawyer, then invited Babaji to Alwar. He was a trustee of the trust that had been set up by Mahendra Maharajji. Shraddhanandji lived in Malan ki Gali at Alwar. Babaji received a glittering reception at his house. The following day, Babaji decided to visit the holy sites Bhartrihari and Pandupol, which were quite close by. There was also a Kaal Bhairav temple near Bhartrihari, where He made His first halt.

There, He directed Shraddhanandji to arrange ghee, milk, yogurt, Ganga jal and *boora* (crushed sugar). Devotees, in the meanwhile, were instructed to walk to the Bhartrihari tomb while the current proceedings were underway. Babaji anointed the idol of Kaal Bhairav with water, Ganga jal, ghee, milk and curd. Shastriji, Shraddhanandji and I were present.

Babaji said, 'Ask for anything you want. This Bhairav will now give you whatever you wish.'

But all we could ask for was Babaji's continuous grace upon us.

Dusk had fallen by the time we reached the Hanuman temple at Pandupol, which stood bang in the middle of Sariska forest. We were told that this was tiger terrain. There was an interesting history attached to the temple. It is said that the Pandavas stayed on a nearby hill and Bhima had paved a pathway with his mace, which exists to this day.

The temple priest received Babaji warmly. We were to stay here for the night. Shraddhanandji had made all the arrangements for our accommodation. Kirtan continued in the temple courtyard after the *Hanuman Chalisa*. Suddenly, Babaji got up and ordered us all to stay where we were. He was going into the forest. Yashpal Rana, the younger son of Fakiranandji, accompanied Him with an *aasan*.

They did not return for quite some time and we all panicked. An hour had passed, but Babaji did not come and neither did Yashpal. All of us were reciting the *Hanuman Chalisa* loudly. We were all worried, fearing the worst. I too was nervous, but I knew that Lord Haidakhan was the living God and no one could do anything to Him.

Then, all of a sudden, we spotted Babajii slowly emerging out of the forest with Yashpal. Our relief was intense. We shouted joyously and greeted their return with frenzied cheers.

After Babaji retired for the night, I asked Yashpal, 'Where did you go with Babaji tonight?'

Other devotees gathered around and sat down near us to hear his tale.

He said, 'Babaji took me into the jungle, and then we started climbing up a hill. After a while we reached the hilltop. I put an *aasan* for Him on a large boulder and He sat down. I too sat a short distance away. All of a sudden, I saw lights flying from the sky. They were gliding towards Maharaj. They sailed from the sky to His feet and then vanished. I timidly asked Him, "What is this Babaji?" He said, "They are coming for someone's darshan." Many such lights came floating in a round circle towards Babaji's feet and disappeared.'

At the time, the incident was avidly discussed. The general consensus among devotees was that the gods and goddesses must have come down for Babaji's darshan in the form of lights. Every aspect of His *leela* was thrashed out and debated threadbare. Yashpal Rana today is located in Delhi, where he works in Dr VVS Rao's office.

The next morning, we returned to Alwar after we'd bathed. We were there for around three days and then went back to Vrindavan. A few days later, Babaji decided that it was time to go back to Haidakhan.

We reached Haldwani at 8 a.m. and the station was literally choked with Babaji's followers. We went to Trilok Singh's house, where the influx of devotees continued unabated. Sages and saints were a common sight at his residence in any case, as he had great faith in them.

Apart from holding a transport job, Trilok Singh owned a bus as well. He was also responsible for transporting the bulk of the vegetables and fruits from the mountains at the time. In addition, he ran his shop, Hind Grain Traders, at Patel Chowk in Haldwani.

We used to send letters from Haidakhan to him to forward, and he used to send flour, pulses, fruits, vegetables, and other items to the ashram on horseback. Horses were the only means of transport to Haidakhan in those days.

How then did Trilok Singh, a transporter and shopkeeper, become Maha Muniraj? The answer, dear readers is—over time and by the grace of Babaji.

49

BABAJI: THE ALL-KNOWING ONE

After a day's halt at Haldwani, we proceeded to Haidakhan in the morning. I had asked Muniraj to organize jeeps to drop us all to Vijaypur. He also arranged horses to transport our goods to the ashram. By the time we reached Haidakhan via Okhaldhunga, the day was almost over.

Babaji was to spend some time in Haidakhan now.

Footfalls of foreign devotees started swelling. Trilok Singh would also come over to see Babaji at least two to three times in a month, usually accompanied by Chacha Amar Singh, Padmadutt Pant, Ramesh Bhatt, Bachhi Singh and Adhikariji.

The walls around the temple had been built. While going down to the river one day, Babaji told Trilok Singh, 'Trilokji, we will now construct stairs to the river. Send over the cement, iron and other items from Haldwani. We will take the stones from the river.'

The village headman Harak Singh Sabhapati and Chandramani of Haidakhan were asked to bring in some local labour. A few artisans were also roped in for the task, and that is how the construction of the stairs to the river began. Devotees were also pressed into service to contribute to the process of collecting stones.

One morning, Babaji looked very grave and did not drink the milk I had prepared for Him.

I asked, 'Maharaj, what is the matter, have I done something wrong?'

He was quiet. I asked again if I had erred in some way, and He replied, 'Today, the King of Nepal, one of our devotees, is no more.'

There was no radio in Haidakhan. How did he know? The newspapers were always delivered a couple of days late at the ashram, so I kept my counsel and waited.

Two days later, I read the news in black and white—King Mahendra of Nepal was dead.

50

THE PRIDE OF POSSESSION

When I was in Vrindavan, my sister sent me a sweater made of white wool. My brother Shivcharanji brought it for me when he came for a visit. I was thrilled and wore it with great joy.

Babaji noticed my pride and said, 'Birju, we don't like that sweater, give it to Pandeyji.'

Revadhar Pandey, who hailed from Almora, served as the priest of the Vrindavan temple at the time. I did not wear the sweater the following day, but neither did I give it to Pandeyji.

The next day, Babaji asked me whether I had given the sweater to Pandeyji. I shook my head and said, 'No, Prabhu.'

He said, 'So, you love your sweater more than us.'

'No, Prabhu, I love you more,' I replied, much chastened.

'Then give the sweater to Pandeyji,' He ordered.

I bowed humbly and quietly handed over the offending garment to Pandeyji with a heavy heart. When the deed was done, He asked Seth Lakshminarayanji to bring me a khadi sweater. A short time later, I was the proud owner of a half-sleeved khadi sweater.

Babaji said, 'Take it, Birju, and wear it.'

I wore it on the way to Haidakhan.

From Haidakhan, we were to go to Nainital for a few days, where Colonel Jeevanchand Joshiji had organized a programme so that devotees there could receive Babaji's darshan. Hemchand Bhatt, an advocate, and Rajendra Shah and Shastriji were with us.

In Nainital, Babaji decided to visit Rajendra Shah, Fakiranandji's son-in-law. I overheard Him asking Rajendra Shah to 'bring four nice jerseys' from the woollen store below his house. When the said sweaters were brought, Babaji said, 'Birju, take these jerseys.'

Frightened, I refused. 'What will I do with them, Prabhu?'

But Babaji insisted.

Unsure of how to react, I said, 'Babaji, give it to someone who you think is good.'

Shastriji stepped in and picked out an olive-green sweater that reminded me of the military. 'Wear this,' he said, and I did. It must be mentioned here that for two years, Babaji Himself did not wear any woollens. He gradually started wearing them a lot later, and that too only after much urging from His devotees.

51

ON TOUR AGAIN

Time went by. I went to Bharatpur to take my exams and returned to Haidakhan after fifteen days. Babaji said, 'Birju, don't worry, you will pass.'

He decided to go to Vrindavan and announced, 'We will stay at Chacha Amar Singh's house in Haldwani.'

Amar Singh Chacha was a man of upright nature who stayed far away from petty human failings like treachery. Babaji sometimes made him deliver discourses. He often carried pilgrims in his trucks to Haidakhan via Jamrani dam and accorded them a lot of respect in his house. His wife too was a very pious person, always happy to welcome devotees to her home and feed them various dishes which she prepared with her own hands. Babaji especially loved to partake of buttermilk prepared by her. His children were also very gentle. Amar Singh Chacha is now gone, but she is still there, though very old.

We reached Haldwani in the afternoon and went to his house. All the local devotees thronged there to see Babaji. On the third day, in the evening, we left Haldwani. The train reached Mathura Cantonment the next morning, and we headed to Vrindavan.

Babaji was scheduled to visit Danta, where He was to perform the Srimad Devi Bhagwatam yagna. A request to that effect had been made by Prithvi Singhji, the Maharaja of Danta. Raghuveer Singh, who was related to the Maharaja, came to Vrindavan to pick up Babaji. Muniraj had also arrived there from Haldwani, and Shastriji came from Rajgarh. While driving us to Danta, Raghuveerji informed us that we would stop over at Pali that day as it was on our way.

We reached Pali in the evening via Jaipur and Ajmer. Phulendra Kumari, Maharaj Prithvi Singhji's sister, lived here. Her husband Narayan Singh was the Superintendent of Police and had arranged our stay at a guest house. Phulendra Kumari had met Babaji earlier in Jaipur, and she now performed His puja with all due rituals.

We left for Danta in the morning, and when we reached, we found the whole palace swamped with devotees. They had got wind of Babaji's plans and had landed there from various places. Jayashree Vora and Dinu Gilder had come with their families from Bombay.

Maharaja Prithviraj Singh's palace stood on top of a hill. It had a lot of rooms and a huge hall on the ground floor. Arrangements had been made to house some of us in these rooms. The Devi Bhagwatam Katha was to take place in the hall. Shastriji, Munirajji and I were to stay here with Lord Haidakhan. Other devotees had been housed in an accommodation that was about a kilometre away and was part of the Maharaja's sprawling estate.

When Babaji entered the palace, Maharani Padmini welcomed Him with Maharaja Prithviraj. She belonged to the princely state of Bikaner, Rajasthan. A chamber had been prepared on the ground floor for Babaji, and Shastriji was to be with Him. Trilok Singh and I were sharing a room close by. The palace was exquisite.

We rose at four in the morning and prepared for the day. Shastriji came to our room for a bath. I started preparing *chandan*. After Babaji had bathed, He applied *chandan* on all of us (Shastriji, Trilokji, the Maharaja and his family). After that, He sat in meditation. In those days, He used to sit in meditation for about two hours after waking up, although earlier, He would meditate for a much longer period.

Shastriji and the Maharaja were involved in a deep discussion regarding the preparation of the puja and havan. At eight in the morning, we set off for the old palace by car, where the Shrimad Devi Bhagwatam Katha had been organized. It was an older part of his royal estate. Several members of his family still resided there.

In the hall, Shastriji's *aasan* had been placed next to Babaji's and a puja sthal (place of worship) had been made for various deities. Shastriji helped the host and hostess perform the prayers in keeping with tradition. He then began the recitation of the Bhagwatam in Sanskrit. This set the pattern for the days to come. He would read the Bhagwatam in Sanskrit till eleven in the morning and would return at 4 p.m. to deliver a discourse on it in Hindi.

People from nearby places like Ambaji were thrilled to receive Babaji's darshan. At night, Babaji would go to the top of the palace with the Maharaja and Maharani for a satsang on the terrace. Shastriji would recount interesting tales about Lord Haidakhan's *leelas*. There were very few scholars like Shastriji at that time. He responded to everything and foretold the future of devotees with the help of a silver amulet that was tied on his wrist with a black string. He fondly called it his personal TV!

In the meanwhile, Trilokji and I were at loggerheads. He used to smoke bidis and it bothered me. I would either hide his bundle of bidis or break them into pieces, and at times I would even throw the whole lot out. I also threatened to tell Babaji that he smoked. We finally arrived at a compromise. He agreed to limit his smoking to just twice a day—once in the morning and once in evening. Later, he quit altogether.

One day, Babaji took all His devotees to Ambaji, which had been part of the Danta State pre-Independence. After the completion of the Srimad Bhagwatam, the yagna was over, and devotees took Babaji's blessings and left.

After the yagna at Danta, we returned to Vrindavan. On the way back, Babaji stayed at Amolak Chand Jain's house in Jaipur. His wife was an ardent devotee of Babaji. He used to live at Kailash Marg in Bani Park, and the family ran a restaurant on contract at Gem Talkies. Babaji was greeted tumultuously by hundreds of devotees when we arrived at the Jain residence.

The next day, He asked the women to deck Amolakji's head with flowers. He asked Shastriji to place him on an *aasan*. Maharaj put His hand on his head and announced, 'He will make predictions today.'

Amolakji began to speak. He prophesied that by the grace of God, the coming time would be very bad. 'Many calamities will take place; men will look at men and die. God will be our only protection. The hardships of these times will only be avoided by chanting "*Om Namah Shivay*". India will be an all-powerful country.'

52

SHASTRIJI: FROM RAJ MISR TO TULSI DAS

We were back at Vrindavan from Jaipur, and Shastriji had an interesting tale to narrate about Mahendra Baba. 'Swamiji once came to Rajgarh and in the evening he took me to the Hanuman temple,' he recalled. 'Standing in front of me was a very real-looking idol of Lord Hanuman. He put his hand on my head and said, "*Jai Jai Jai Hanuman Gusain Kripa Karo Gurudev kinaeen*". He said these words from the *Hanuman Chalisa* thrice, and Hanumanji Himself appeared. I was terrified and touched His feet. He patted me thrice on my head and said, "*Om Shanti, Shanti, Shanti*".' I knew that Shri Mahendra Maharajji was the incarnation of Goddess Amba or Durga. But after that day, Her sister, Goddess Saraswati, started living on my tongue and whatever I said turned into couplets.'

After a few days, Mahendra Babaji left. Shastriji told me, 'I was earlier the raj purohit (royal priest) of the King of Alwar, Maharaja Pratap Singh. He presented me Atal Dasji's temple and its land at Rajgarh near Alwar. Maharaja Pratap Singh was a Ram devotee and asked me to depict Lord Shri Ram's inner *leela* the way Raskhan, the sixteenth century poet, had portrayed Lord Krishna's inner *leela*.'

53

LOST IN THE WOODS

After staying in Vrindavan for a few days, Babaji thought it was time to go back to Haidakhan.

On the way, I remarked, 'Prabhu, you stay a lot in Vrindavan.'

He responded, 'Birju, there are a lot of devotees who cannot come to Haidakhan. I go to various places and stay at Vrindavan to fulfil their desire for darshan.'

This time, we stayed with Ram Prakash Bhasinji in Haldwani. The Bhasin family were devout followers of Babaji. Here too, all the local devotees congregated for His darshan. The next day, we went to Haidakhan via Vijaypur chowk.

Babaji had very soft feet despite the fact that He had walked barefoot for many years. I remember Him walking barefoot to Mount Kailash too; the devotees who accompanied Him also went unshod. He told them that they could wear shoes or slippers, but they refused. Babaji laughed and said, 'Well, the number of stones that hurt your feet will be directly proportional to the number of your sins that are destroyed!'

One day, He said, 'Birju, I want to go to Siddheshwar. Nar Narayan performed their austerities there.'

Siddheshwar was on the other side of the Adi Kailash. He turned to His devotees and asked, 'Who wants to come with Us?'

Was it possible that any devotee would refuse? They all said they did. People from Haidakhan village also agreed to go. Chandan Singh, his father Govardhan Singh, Harak Singh, Chandramani and his sons, all said they would accompany Him on the trek. Babaji said, 'We will stay there for the night.'

I took some fruits, clothes and *chandan*, and we started the trek to Siddheshwar. Chandramaniji's house was on the way. We had breakfast there. He had not brought milk and curd to Haidakhan for Babaji that day, so He drank some milk there and then we resumed our trek. We reached Siddheshwar at around four in the evening. Many devotees from nearby villages were already there to welcome us with yogurt, milk and fruits.

Several fires had been lit. Beds of grass had been laid at several places. Devotees gratefully sat down on them. A separate grass bed had been made for Babaji near a small temple. I placed His *aasan* on it, which I had carried with me all the way from Haidakhan. A meal of aloo-puris had been cooked for all of us in copious quantities by local devotees. Chandramaniji had apparently relayed the news of Babaji's arrival beforehand. The burning fires chased away the cold, and the kirtan began.

At 8 p.m. Babaji ordered everyone to eat. I went to fetch His milk and gave it to Him in a steel *lutiya*, a small drinking vessel.

A retired seventy-year-old railway guard, Gangashaya Med, who was a devotee of Mahendra Maharaj, had come along with us for the trip. Babaji said, 'Birju, you and the guard sleep here near me.'

Medji and I lay down on the grass. Despite the open sky, the bonfire kept us warm. In the morning, I bowed to Babaji and prepared to head for my bath. He was just about to sit in meditation when He stopped me. 'There's no need to take a bath here, the pure air here cleanses a person.'

Later in the morning, after everyone was up and about, Babaji said, 'We should get ready to go back to Haidakhan.'

Local devotees had arranged tea for everyone. We had some and then, at around 7 a.m., we commenced on our return journey. Babaji said, 'Birju, you stay close to Medji.' He handed the old man a stick and said, 'Hold this and come down slowly.'

I walked down slowly with the guard, keeping a close watch on him. He was elderly and the descent was a struggle for him. Babaji went ahead, with the other devotees close on His heels.

Age apart, guard sahib was also weak. Gradually, Babaji and the others disappeared from sight. The entire trek to Siddheshwar was densely forested. After trudging across the wooded trail for a long time, we took off on the wrong path and lost our way. At some point, it dawned on us that we had gone astray. The fear of encountering some wild animal started preying on our minds.

'Why don't we go towards the river,' I suggested to Medji.

He was open to the idea. I parted the shrubbery with a stick to carve out a path and we pressed ahead through the woods at a snail's pace. He was tiring out; the walk was obviously taking a toll on him. At some places, we almost slipped over the slopes and only escaped rolling over by the skin of our teeth; at others, we had to turn back because there was no proper pathway, and there were some spots where we had to brave thickets of thorns that left scratches on our legs and feet. We still forged ahead stoically.

I sent up a silent prayer to Babaji, entreating a rescue, unaware that He had already figured out that we were lost. He had worked out our location and had dispatched Govardhan Singh to fetch us. In the meanwhile, invoking His name, we trekked onwards and finally landed on the banks of the river at about 3 p.m. Just then, I espied Govardhanji at a distance. Our nightmare was over.

I hailed him loudly and he greeted us cheerfully, very pleased to see us. He brought us up to date. Babaji had been very worried about us. He had waited at Chandramaniji's house for a long time, before dispatching Govardhanji to find us. He had left for Haidakhan Ashram after issuing the following instruction. 'Stay here and wait. Bring them to the ashram when you find them.'

The rest of the walk was relatively easy, as Govardhanji was familiar with the route. Babaji was waiting for us at the ashram. He laughed when He saw us and asked, 'Where have you been?'

When I narrated the tale of our adventure, He said, 'That's why we left you with the guard.'

I responded philosophically, 'I knew it was all your *leela*.'

Medji addressed Babaji with folded hands. 'Prabhu, I will not go on any journey from now on. I will serve you while staying at Haidakhan.'

The guard was a very honest and kind man who insisted on donating his entire pension to the ashram. On many occasions, Babaji tried to forbid him, but he would pay no heed. All he would say was, 'It's all yours.'

Guard sahib used to keep track of all the labour and any work that was done at Haidakhan. He also took care of all the transactions. Babaji offered him a small room to live in, in front of the mausoleum. Now he is no longer there. When Babaji travelled, Medji would stay back and look after the ashram.

One day, Babaji said, 'Birju, you have too much work on your plate. You're not only cooking for those in the ashram, but also for the sadhus who come here. You even have to sweep the place when there are no devotees. Why don't we employ someone to help you in your work?'

I said, 'Okay.'

It was 1973. That evening, Prabhu caught hold of a timber contractor and said, 'We need a good person for the ashram.'

A number of Nepali labourers worked for him. The following day, the contractor brought Man Singh and said, 'Babaji, this person is from my community. Please employ him.'

Babaji called me and said, 'Birju, keep this person with you. He will help you. Teach him how to work.'

Man Singh turned out to be a great find. He was very hard working and courageous. He started helping me with my work. He stayed on at Haidakhan Ashram and served it with great devotion. He lives there even today after his retirement. It's very hard to find an honest and hardworking person like him in this day and age. He stayed with Babaji as long as He was in His body.

54

TO THE VILLAGE OF DHANIYAN AND BACK

Babaji and I went to a village called Dhaniyan in Almora with some devotees in tow. Shastriji was also with us. The approach to the village was difficult, as it went through some very unfriendly mountainous terrain ascending almost all the way to the Chitai temple. From there, it sloped down to a river that had to be crossed. On the other side, another upward ascent began through a mud track that went right up to what appeared to be a hamlet to my unappreciative eyes.

There was a small settlement here, where Fakiranandji's elder brother Dilip Rana lived. Fakiranandji himself worked in Delhi, and a Shrimad Devi Bhagwatam Katha had already taken place there under Babaji's watchful eye at his residence in Inderpuri, in 1971. A lot of people from the Pusa Institute had come for Babaji's darshan, one of them being Ved Prakash Tiwari (christened Mahant Baba by Babaji), who travelled from place to place to serve Him.

I remember once when he came to Vrindavan, Babaji asked him to get his head tonsured. Ved Prakashji tried to duck His orders, but his wife objected. 'How can you ignore Babaji's orders? You must obey Him.'

Ved Prakashji finally yielded and unenthusiastically went and had his head shaved. Anyone could see that his heart was not in it. Now, he has built a temple dedicated to Babaji in Janakpuri and is still serving Him. He has even written books on Babaji.

In Dhaniyan, I think Fakiranandji's house had fourteen rooms; more could not be built. There is an interesting mystery attached to this. On the first floor, there was a room for Babaji which overlooked a small verandah where bedding had been laid for Shastriji and me. Nearby, there was a spring where we used to go and bathe. Very close to it, the family deities were said to live in a sacred space. Pouring out his woes to Babaji, Farkiraji told Him that an evil soul had started haunting the place and it was hindering the prosperity of the family. No additional constructions could be made to his house. In the morning, Babaji went to the spring for a bath and I started preparing the *chandan*.

After staying at Dhaniyan for a few days, we went back to Haidakhan. On the way, Shastriji composed a couplet and began to recite it to Babaji. '*Dhanya Dhanya* Dhaniyan, *Jahan mile na supari paan, Jahan Pragate Ranaji jaise Bhaktmahan*' (Blessed, Blessed Dhaniyan, where you get neither betel nut nor betel leaf, but where appear great devotees like Ranaji). Babaji burst out laughing. It tickled our funny bone so much that we kept singing the couplet repeatedly till we reached the ashram.

Those were the days, when the temple at Chilianaula, Ranikhet, had not been built. After we reached Haidakhan, Babaji headed to the cave for his evening bath. 'There'll be as many devotees here one day, Birju, as there are stones in the river,' He said as He left.

He had said this to me once before, when we had just arrived at Haidakhan. I knew His words would come true, and they did. The number of devotees visiting Haidakhan grew so large that several tents had to be pitched by the river. There came a time when every time I turned, I encountered a devotee.

Shastriji went off to Rajgarh from Haldwani, and after some time, we left for Vrindavan. There too, the story was the same, and we kept encountering an unending influx of devotees. Among those who converged to meet Babaji was Vijay Bhatiani, a devout disciple of Babaji who frequently dropped in from Delhi to meet Him.

On this occasion, he had brought along Dr SK Lal and his wife, Vimla Mataji, for Babaji's darshan. After introducing them to Babaji, he also went to Madhuban. Vijayji had a very quiet disposition and spoke even less than Babaji did. His affection for me was tremendous and his wife Meeraji too was very fond of me. In fact, his entire family had a soft spot for me. He treats me with the same warmth even today.

55

NEW LEELA

It was December 1973. A new *leela* was about to begin in my life. One day, my mother came to Vrindavan and started crying. She told Babaji, 'I do not want my son to become a Baba. My spirit resides in him.'

I was the youngest in the family. My father and an elder sister had died when I was a child. My two elder brothers and an elder sister were married. I also had one sister who was still single and who often wept because she missed me. I was saddened by my mother's distress and felt very conflicted. On one hand, there was Lord Haidakhan, whom I venerated and did not want to leave, and on the other, there was my mother who had given birth to me.

Lord Haidakhan told her, 'Go for now, we'll do something soon.'

She had come with my brother Shivcharan, who was extremely devoted to Babaji. He was also very unique in his thought process. He did not want me to leave Babaji.

Babaji did not say anything on that first day. The next day, however, He summoned me to His room and said, 'Birju, what have you thought? Your mother's sad face has been haunting us.'

I was torn and confused. I wondered if my salvation would be possible without Him. Should I tell Him that my time with Him was at an end? There was a part of my mind which was turning towards home. I was still in a dilemma when Babaji said, 'Birju, do not be disappointed. You are always with us. We are saddened by the agony of your mother. Go home and serve her. You can always keep on visiting us. Our blessings will always be with you. How fortunate you are to have served us at this young age!'

He took out a bundle of clothes and some money and said, 'Birju, keep this, as it will be useful.'

I folded my hands and said, 'These offerings have been made by your devotees. Would it even be proper for me to accept them from you? I want nothing but your blessings.'

Babaji laughed and said, 'We expected nothing else from you.'

I came out of His room and grieved. I packed my things, took leave of the other devotees and went back to Bharatpur.

It was my good fortune that He wrote about thirty-one great personalities, like Vikramaditya, in this incarnation. He has described whoever was with Him in His modern-day *leela* in the *Sadashiv Charitamrit* in *Sudha Kalash*.

In couplet number 558, Babaji has written about me: '*Bijiyapati, Sri Vijayji, karein sada gungaan, priye sevak prabhu ke, pratham chela, maha mahaan*,' meaning Sri Vijay always praises Bijyapati i.e., Lord Shiva. He is the prime servitor of the lord, dearly beloved to him; he is very great.

56

TRILOK SINGHJI BECOMES MAHA MUNIRAJ

In 1974, when Babaji performed a yagna at Kudesia Ghat on the banks of the Yamuna in Delhi, He placed a takht at a short distance from His own *aasan* and seated Trilok Singhji on the takht. Babaji directed all the devotees who came to Him to also pay obeisance to 'the big saint sitting there. He is called Maha Muniraj'. It became the accepted practice; everyone who bowed to Babaji would then head to Maha Muniraj for his blessings, and hundreds of devotees started visiting him. Dr SK Lal, our present Chairman Dr Arvind Lal's late father, was especially asked to arrange exotic meals for Muniraj from one of Delhi's famous restaurants—Gaylord!

One day, the head of the Delhi branch of Bhrigu Durbar (a religious organization specializing in astrological predictions passed down from the saint Bhrigu, with branches all over the country) came to visit Babaji at the Kudesia ghat and bowed to Him.

Babaji told him to go to Maha Muniraj. 'He who is sitting there is an even bigger saint than we are!'

The man was accompanied by several devotees and, at Babaji's prodding, they all sought Munirajji's blessings as well. The visit sparked fervid discussions among the Bhrigu Durbar devotees who thought that Babaji must be a very holy personage indeed, since their guru had bowed to Him in front of his own devotees. Several of them shifted allegiance to Babaji.*

---

* It was already foretold in the *Brighu Samhita* that Lord Shiv will appear in the form of Haidakhan Baba in Kalyug.

57

PANWAR SAHIB

I came back to Bharatpur and completed my graduation and later did an LLB from Rajasthan University. By Babaji's grace, I kept passing all my exams. By now, a lot of foreigners had started coming to Babaji. I too would often go to Haidakhan.

After my departure, Chakleshwar and priest Hiralal started serving Babaji. Hiralalji was the priest at the Vrindavan temple.

Shastriji had retired. He spent most of his time serving Babaji. He would read new books to Babaji and often slept in His room. One day, he caught hold of me and said, 'Birju, there is a book, *Aag Aur Paani* by Raghuveer Sharan Mishr, which I have been desperately looking for. Please find it for me. Many people were put on the job, but no one could find it. These are Prabhu's orders.'

I kept hunting for the book all over, and finally after a long and seemingly endless search, I found it in a bookshop beneath the Madras Hotel in Connaught Place, Delhi. When I presented the book to Babaji, He was triumphant. He looked at Shastriji and commented, 'I told you that Birju would definitely find it and bring it from somewhere.'

Whenever Babaji went to Bombay by car, I would welcome Him with a lot of people at Bharatpur. It was always my desire that, since Babaji represented truth, everyone should benefit from His darshan.

Once, when He was coming to Mathura from Bombay, He told me to inform the Superintendent of Police Samarveer Singh Panwar, who belonged to the royal family of Tehri, of His arrival. Panwar sahib enjoyed a sterling reputation in the Bharatpur region for his honesty and nobility of character. He was also feared by the police administration.

Samarveerji's mother was Babaji's devotee. She was a relative of the Rajguru (royal guru) of Nepal. I remember when Babaji went with His devotees to Nepal (I also had the privilege of going along), the Rajguru of Nepal laid out the red carpet for Him. He not only arranged food and lodging for Babaji's devotees but also housed Babaji at his own residence. Everyone accompanied Babaji to the Pashupatinath temple during that trip; the priests there showed Him some valuables, among them a ruby, which belonged to the deity.

Aware of his reputation, I nervously went to his residence to deliver Babaji's message. He said, 'My mother is His devotee. I will tell Rani sahiba, and I will also try to come to the station.'

Paschim Express used to arrive at Bharatpur in the morning those days. I was waiting at the station with some devotees. As Shivcharan bhaisahib was in the railways, he usually managed to delay the train a bit longer than its scheduled halt.

Just then, I saw Panwar sahib coming to the platform with his mother. There were a lot of policemen with him. After a while, the train arrived at the platform. Babaji was standing at the door of the AC compartment to give darshan to His devotees. '*Bhole Babaji ki Jai*', His devotees yelled.

Panwar sahib came forward to pay homage to Babaji with his mother. While blessing them, He ordered me to tell Panwar sahib and his mother to come to Vrindavan the next day. The SP sahib heard me out and held his peace.

Once the train departed, everyone started trickling out of the station to return home. Just as I was leaving, Panwar sahib asked me to meet him at his house in the evening. I reached his residence, where besides his mother, his wife Preeti was also present. She belonged to the Jodhpur royal family.

Panwar sahib said, 'Look, Vijay, I don't have too much faith in Babas. My mother is the one who is His devotee. She will go with you to Vrindavan. I will arrange a car. Come here in the morning. In any case, the IG, Mr Ganesh Singh, is currently here. We are going for an inspection to the Deeg and Kaman police stations tomorrow. Please convey my apologies to Babaji.'

When I went to pick up his mother in the morning, he said, 'Vijay, a very strange thing has happened. I just got a call from the IG sahib's wife to tell me that he will not be carrying out any inspections today as he is going to a temple in Vrindavan for darshan.'

I was stunned. How had this happened? He ignored my surprise and continued, 'I will be accompanying him. But I don't know if I'll be able to squeeze time to meet Babaji.'

I escorted his mother to Vrindavan. Babaji was sitting outside and a kirtan was going on. Babaji made Rani sahiba sit near his *aasan*. 'Panwar sahib hasn't come?' He asked. I told him what the SP had told me.

Half an hour later, a UP police car arrived. Babaji said to me, 'Ask them what's the matter.'

I approached the cops and asked, 'What's the matter?'

A policeman replied, 'Kaptaan Sahib Bharatpur has come to meet Babaji.'

I gaped at him open-mouthed. Just then, I spotted Panwar sahib climbing up the temple stairs with a garland in his hands. He bowed to Babaji and said, 'I am on duty. I came to Vrindavan with IG sahib. I asked him for some time off so that I could come and see you.'

Babaji lovingly gave him some prasad and when Panwarji took his leave, He said, 'See off SP sahib outside.'

The SP had barely taken a few steps forward when Babaji threw a garland at him. It fell around his neck. Taken by surprise, Panwar sahib looked back. Very quickly, he recovered his poise, smiled and walked away. Babaji always treated His guests with love and respect and took great care of them.

We returned to Bharatpur after receiving prasad at the Vrindavan temple. Panwar sahib's encounter with Babaji left such a deep impression on him that he even visited Babaji at Haidakhan with me. Whenever Babaji went to Bombay via Kota by train, Panwar sahib would go to the station for His darshan.

Once, on his way to Jaipur, Babaji stopped at his residence in Bharatpur, and Panwar sahib then worshipped Babaji at the Shiva temple in Police Lines. Panwar sahib and his wife became so fond of me that I would visit them regularly, at least once every two days. As long as he was alive, he would call up any SP or DIG who was posted at Bharatpur and tell them that I was his like his younger brother; consequently, they would all treat me with great courtesy. As a result, over time, I came in touch with several top officers in the police department.

After he was transferred to Kota from Bharatpur, he got me a job at JK Synthetics. While I was in Kota, he made sure that I always had a police car and two policemen at my disposal. I would go for meetings to senior managers escorted by the police establishment, and matters went on this way for fifteen days. I sent a letter to Babaji informing Him of my new job.

A few days later, I received a letter from Fakiranandji. He wrote and told me that Babaji had not created me to become a servant. He wanted me to quit the job. I was in a muddle. What would I tell SP sahib? I finally just left for Bharatpur without informing Samarveerji. When he found out, he called Mr Mohan Singh Bhati, Additional Superintendent of Police, Bharatpur, and said, 'Tell Vijay to talk to me, and send him to Kota.'

Two policemen landed up at my house and said, 'Bhati sahib has called you.'

I was rattled by their visit as I did not know what was wrong. The then sitting MP from our constituency, Pandit Ramkishan, lived near my house and my family was on close terms with him. I went to him fearfully and apprised him of the situation. 'Can you please call Bhati sahib and ask him what's the matter?'

Pandit Ramkishan called up Bhati sahib and said, 'Why are you calling Vijay?'

Bhati sahib said, 'I have a message for Vijay from Panwar sahib. Tell him to come to my house in the evening.'

That evening, I went to Bhatiji's house. He received me very courteously and told me that SP sahib was calling me to Kota. I asked him if I could speak to Panwar sahib over the phone. He dialled the number and put me through. I talked to Samarveerji and told him about Babaji's decree.

'You should have told me earlier,' he said mildly. I apologized. Our relationship survived the incident and remained intact. Even after Babaji took samadhi, Samarveerji and his wife always helped me.

58

BABAJI PLAYS MATCHMAKER

I was returning from Vapi with Babaji. The first-class bogey was fully booked and devotees had grabbed seats wherever they could find them. A young woman was also travelling in the same compartment. She was an ayurvedic doctor on her way home to Baroda. She ventured into the coupe where Babaji was sitting with Shastriji to inquire what the stars foretold of her marriage and the year that it would take place.

'We will get you married right now,' Babaji replied.

Maharaj asked Shastriji to call me. Grinning from ear to ear, he came up to me and said, 'Babaji is calling you.'

When I reached the door, I saw a girl of about twenty-five or twenty-six standing in the compartment. She was about five feet two inches tall and slightly rotund. Still unsuspecting, I entered the compartment.

Babaji quickly shut the door of the coupe and grabbed my hand. He said, 'Shastriji, chant the mantras, we will marry Birju to this girl.'

Outraged, I kept refusing, declaring that I would not accept the marriage. Babaji as usual ignored me and queried, 'How will you not accept the marriage?'

Shastriji kept on chanting mantras.

'Go lock them in a coupe,' Babaji said to a devotee after the faux-wedding rituals were complete.

The girl obediently went into a coupe that had been emptied out for us, but I fled and kept running from bogey to bogey trying to shake off my pursuers. It was only when I learnt that the girl had got off at Baroda did I return to the compartment, only to find myself the butt of many jokes among the devotees.

I later asked Babaji why He had made me undergo that mock-marriage. He responded with a laugh, 'Birju, the situation was such that if we had not carried out the mock-ceremony, then the girl would have never got married. We removed the hurdles to her marriage.'

I dismissed the incident from my mind, but the girl had obviously taken the ceremony seriously. When Babaji took samadhi, she came to Bharatpur to ask me about my intentions. I told her that since I had not accepted the marriage when He was alive, there was no way I would accept it now.

Something about her mien tugged at me, and I tried to soften the blow. 'It was Babaji's *leela*,' I explained. I then told her why Babaji had made us undergo the mock-marriage. 'It was to remove the *dosh* (unfavourable condition or position of planets in Vedic astrology) that was preventing your marriage.'

Several years later, I learnt that she had married someone else and was now running her own hospital and living a happy life with her husband.

When Babaji yielded to my mother's pleadings and dispatched me back to Bharatpur, He had said, 'Birju, do not be disappointed. You are always with us. We are saddened by the agony of your mother. Go home and serve her. You can always keep on visiting us.' He was on the dot. I went back home to Bharatpur, but He was always with me and whenever I missed Him, I went to Him no matter where He was.

In 1976, I took off from Bharatpur for Haidakhan. At Haldwani, I discovered that Babaji was at the Khanna farm performing a yagna for an old lady who was popularly known as Khanna Mataji, because the family originally hailed from Khanna Village in Punjab.

Khanna Mataji was a wise, compassionate and peace-loving woman. There were two such old ladies in Haldwani at that time. One was the lady under discussion, and the other was Kichcha Mataji. Babaji respected them both. A third lady who commanded his esteem was Vimla Mataji (Dr Arvind Lal's mother). She hailed from Delhi.

I landed up at Muniraj's house, and he took me to Khanna farm to meet Babaji. When Babaji saw me, He was surprised. 'When did you come? And how did you find out I was here?'

'Muniraj told me,' I replied chirpily. I was thrilled to bits that I was with Babaji again.

It set the pattern for the days that followed. In the day, Muniraj and I would go to the Khanna farm, and at night we would return to his house.

One day, I saw a couple at the farm watching the proceedings from a distance. When I asked Muniraj about them, he told me that they were Khanna Mataji's son Lakshmi Ahluwalia and his wife Renu. At that time, they thought Babaji was a charlatan. But they later became deeply devoted to Him. Babaji nicknamed Renuji 'Devi' (Goddess), and Devi she became to all of us.

Devotees kept drifting in from various places from time to time to seek Babaji's blessings and advice. Srivastava Mataji's family had come from Delhi, where her son held a highly paid job. Babaji had a proposal for Srivastava Mataji. 'We want to marry your son to Muniraj's little daughter.'

Muniraj was silent, but Srivastava Mataji said, 'Let me think about it.'

Muniraj's daughter, Devi, was a girl with a great deal of courage. She was also very blunt, though extremely kind. She looked upon me as her elder brother and usually paid heed to what I said. In those days, I used to kip with Muniraj in his room. I told Devi, 'Babaji wants you to get married. The boy is from Delhi.'

She did not respond.

Muniraj was in a quandary but he was constrained by Babaji's wishes and kept silent. We arrived at the Khanna farm in the morning and found a very peculiar atmosphere at play. Srivastava Mataji had apparently put forward some demands, which were conditional to her acceptance of the proposed nuptials. Incensed, Babaji naturally refused and asked them to leave. Still furious, He told Fakiranandji to summon his son to Haldwani as soon as possible. Fakiraji immediately sent a telegram to his son Bhagwan Rana, who was an army officer at the time, and asked him to reach Haldwani in double quick time. 'We will perform the wedding on the same date,' Babaji vowed.

Fakiraji was a resident of Dhaniyan. When Devi learnt of the latest developments, she rebelled and declared that she was not prepared to get married.

Muniraj was in distress. At night he told me, 'You should explain the situation to Devi, because I cannot refuse Babaji's command.'

I promised to have a talk with her. I later sat her down and reasoned with her. I told her that Babaji was a well-wisher and would not wish ill for her. She would also have the luxury of staying with her husband wherever he was posted, unlike a large majority of girls in the hills who were expected to stay with their husbands' parents while their spouses went out of state to work. She heard me out quietly and finally agreed to the marriage. The two were married shortly afterwards with great pomp under Babaji's supervision.

On my next trip, I drew Babaji's wrath. I had gone to Haidakhan for a few days, where a big yagna was being organized on the banks of the Gautami Ganga. Devotees from several states had come to attend it. The day before the yagna, I asked Babaji for permission to leave and, because I persisted, He let me go, but He was not very pleased. I started out from Haidakhan and encountered Muniraj on the way.

He noticed my luggage and realized I was leaving. 'Birju, why are you going in the middle of such a big yagna?' He convinced me that I was making a monumental mistake and brought me back to the ashram.

Babaji was standing below the stairs when we reached Haidakhan. He glared at me and said, 'Birju, why have you come back?'

I told him that Muniraj had convinced me of the error of my ways. Babaji looked even more infuriated. 'When we asked you to stay back, you did not listen, and now you have returned because Muniraj told you that you were wrong! You ignored our orders, so you can leave the ashram boundaries right now!'

I was deeply ashamed and beseeched Him to forgive me. But He was unyielding. Muniraj maintained a politic silence and did not interfere. The idea of trekking down to Haldwani at the close of day was scary, but with no choice left in the matter, a strong streak of obstinacy came to my aid. It sustained me through the long walk back to town; the fact that by a stroke of good luck I also met a local on the way of course helped in no small way to settle my fears.

We reached Jamrani dam at around 9 p.m. where I climbed onto a truck which dropped me to Haldwani. By 10 p.m. I was at Muniraj's house. I spent the night there and left for Bharatpur in the morning. After a while, I got a letter from Fakiraji asking after my health. He wrote, 'Here, Babaji was thinking that you would stay at the cave that night. He is missing you.'

I felt sad. Babaji was like my mother and father rolled into one. Perhaps in this too, He had my welfare in mind.

When later I met up with Babaji at Vrindavan, He told me, 'Birju, we thought that you would stay at the cave that night.'

'Prabhu, you told me to leave the boundaries of Haidakhan. How could I have stayed?' I asked.

'This is what we expected of you,' said Babaji. 'People learnt that while we are fond of you, we can also punish you for refusing to obey our orders so that the others don't make the same mistake.'

He gestured and made me sit near Him and suddenly, all my anger drained away.

I don't remember which festival was going on, but the Rajvaid (royal doctor) had come with me from Bharatpur for Babaji's darshan at Vrindavan. Babaji was sitting on His *aasan*, and the Rajvaid began to ask Him about his daughter's marriage.

Babaji replied, 'Why are you worried? We have already found a boy for your daughter.' He pointed to a young fellow, Prabhat Joshi, who was standing next to him. 'This is the boy. He is very gentle. Go and fetch your daughter.'

Rajvaid went back to Bharatpur but did not return with his daughter the following day. Babaji was still in Vrindavan. When the Rajvaid did not show up, Babaji said, 'Birju, we have to get Prabhat married in Bharatpur. If Rajvaidji does not bring his daughter, then it is up to you to find some other girl.'

I took off to Bharatpur and talked to the Rajvaid. He informed me that his family and daughter were not ready for a marriage in the ashram. I did not go back to Vrindavan. I was too embarrassed. One day soon after, I went to Subhash Sharma's house. He was an engineer in the roadways, and he and his wife had already met Babaji with me, earlier. Subhashji's wife's niece (sister's daughter), Manju, was living with them at that time. She was an extremely simple and innocent girl. I told Subhashji of my dilemma and the sticky situation that I was in, thanks to the Rajvaid.

'What does the boy do and what is his name?' He asked me.

I told him that his name was Prabhat Joshi and that he held a managerial position at a five-star hotel. 'He is good-looking and well-behaved,' I added.

Subhashji liked the sound of him, and I took him to Vrindavan. He told Babaji that he had a girl who was of marriageable age and he was agreeable to the idea of marrying her to Prabhat. Babaji was very happy. He instructed me to get in touch with Naveen Joshi, Prabhat's elder brother, to fix the match.

A clear and forthright person, Naveen had previously held a very high position in Hindustan Motors. He had left his job after he became part of Babaji's entourage. He was not afraid of anyone but Babaji. He had once brought the former Prime Minister of India, Gulzari Lal Nanda, for Babaji's darshan. Nandaji had presented Babaji with a Nagphani (serpentine horn) which He played sometimes.

I took Subhashji to Naveen and apprised him of the proposal. He said, 'Tell Babaji, I don't mind. Prabhat will do whatever Babaji decides.'

We went back to Babaji and told him what Naveen had said. Babaji told us to organize the wedding at Haidakhan and even fixed the date.

I took Manju and her family to Haidakhan. Naveenji had reached before us with Prabhat and the rest of their clan. When we walked into the ashram, he said, 'Vijay, this marriage will not take place.'

I was aghast. 'Why?' I asked.

'Because you were supposed to reach the ashram before us,' was the reply.

When Babaji reiterated Naveen's words, the girl's side became very nervous. I was enraged. I told Babaji, 'Prabhu, it is now time to stop your *leela*.'

Babaji paid no heed, and Naveenji refused to support me.

Babaji turned and started walking from the ashram towards the Haidakhan cave.

'Why are you doing this?' I pleaded. 'My honour will be mud. What will the girl's family think?' I asked.

I knew that Babaji would relent in the end. But when? Why had He devised this latest *leela*?

I kept pestering Him, and just as He started walking down the path to the river, I lost patience and blocked his way.

'Enough of your *leela*,' I said. 'Give orders for the wedding.'

He burst out laughing and said, 'Come on, then. We'll get them married in the cave right now.'

I took Manju to the cave, where her marriage to Prabhat took place in Babaji's presence. Shastriji performed the ceremony with both families in attendance. Subhashji went back to Bharatpur with his family once the nuptial knot had been tied.

59

ANOTHER MIRACLE

I think this incident dates back to 1980. I always wanted more and more devotees to join Babaji. At this time, KK Singh was the Additional Superintendent of Police in Bharatpur. He and his family were devotees of Babaji and would often come for His darshan to Vrindavan. He requested me to take his children along whenever I went to Haidakhan. He had three daughters, and a son whose name was Vivek.

After his stint at Bharatpur, KK Singh was transferred to Jodhpur. His family was upset, because they had been hoping that he would be posted to Dholpur. I went to Haidakhan with his children—all four of them. We reached the ashram by truck at around 4 p.m. Babaji was sitting on a rock in the Gautami Ganga below.

We all bowed to Him, and I introduced Him to KK Singh's offspring. The very next moment, the eldest daughter Prerna stood in front of Babaji and burst into tears.

'What's the matter?' Babaji asked.

She replied that their mother was alone at home and their father had been transferred from Bharatpur to Jodhpur. 'I wanted him to be transferred to Dholpur!' she wailed.

Babaji laughed and said, 'We have transferred him to Dholpur.'

I could see that she had not an iota of doubt in Babaji's words. Babaji asked her brother, who was very gentle, to sit beside Him. In the meanwhile, I went up to arrange for their stay. After some time, Vivek came upstairs with Babaji, and a few days later we headed back to Bharatpur. When I dropped them at their house at the Police Lines, we learned that KK Singh had been posted to Dholpur. Overjoyed by the news, Prerna told her mother what had transpired during her meeting with Babaji.

After they shifted to Dholpur, I met them a couple of times but lost touch with them once Babaji took samadhi.

Nearly thirty-two years later, one day, KK Singh called me. I was surprised but happy to hear from him. He inquired about my whereabouts; I told him. When I asked him where he was located, he said, 'I have settled in Dholpur after retirement. All my children are now married. Prerna is in Jaipur. Her husband is a customs officer. My younger daughter is in Delhi. She's married to a doctor, and Vivek has joined the IAS. He's in the West Bengal cadre and his wife is in the IRS. She is currently posted in Delhi.'

I was very pleased to hear that the kids I had taken to Haidakhan so long ago had fared so well in life. A picture of the way they had been as children darted through my mind.

'Tell me, what made you think of me?' I asked.

'Vijay, we want to go to Haidakhan to see Babaji's samadhi,' KK replied. 'The whole family wants you to go with us.'

I thought it was a lovely idea and said, 'Fix the programme. I'll be happy to go with you.'

Shortly afterwards, I got a call. 'Vijay, we have booked your ticket on the Shatabdi Express. Meet us at the station.'

I met them at the station on the appointed date and time, where he reintroduced me to his children. I was very happy to meet them again and a picture of them as children flashed in my mind again. We reached Kathgodam at 11:30 a.m. Vivek had asked an officer from Nainital to arrange a small minibus for us. We reached Haidakhan at around 2 p.m. I had already arranged their accommodation. After receiving prasad, we all retreated to our rooms for a rest.

After the evening *aarti*, we attended the satsang in the temple. I started telling them about Babaji's various *leelas*. Then they all joined in and began to reminisce over their individual experiences during that first trip to Haidakhan. Prerna talked about their arrival at Haidakhan all those years ago and said, 'You remember when I met Babaji on that trip, I asked for Papa's transfer to Dholpur?' I nodded. 'But do you know what Vivek had asked for that day?'

I shook my head.

Vivek then recounted what had happened when he sat beside Babaji that day. Babaji had told him to stay at the ashram for a few days. At first, he had been shy, but after a bit he had confided in Him. 'I told him that I wanted to join the IAS. Today, by His grace, I am in the IAS. I am now the Education Secretary in Calcutta.'

This piece of information was new to me. I had been unaware of it during our previous stay at Haidakhan. There are some great saints who have the ability to change the fate of human lives. Babaji was obviously one of them. Vivek is currently serving as Principal Secretary, Health in Calcutta. His honesty is a by-word in administrative circles.

His wife Shubha was also with him. She sang hymns to the Lord in a very sweet voice with great piety. She is presently serving as Commissioner, GST in Delhi. Shubha helped in translating the book I wrote into English. She has a very beautiful turn of phrase. In this regard, Pradeep Sen, a retired IAS officer from the Rajasthan cadre, must also find mention here. A former Home Secretary, Sen sahib's contribution to the translation of this book is extremely valuable.

We came back from Haidakhan after a two-day stay. I am still in touch with Prerna, Vivek and Shubha.

60

BABAJI AND THE PILOTS

Babaji once said, 'Birju we want you to preach about us.'

He was on his way back from Bombay, and I had got into His car at Bharatpur. Shastriji was with Him, and we were all going to Delhi to Dr Arvind Lal's house.

'Prabhu,' I replied, 'you're quite capable of doing it yourself. What standing do I have to preach about you? Besides, one thing I do know—no man can know you or come close to you unless you wish it.'

Babaji had fresh instructions for me. 'Birju, bring a member of Parliament to us.'

I thought this was a very strange request. What new *leela* was this! It wasn't as if an MP was some kind of object that I could drag in, and how on earth was I supposed to dig out an MP from somewhere? Babaji guessed my thoughts and simply told me to try. 'You'll be successful.'

We came to Dr Arvind Lal in Delhi and were received very respectfully by his mother and wife. Dr Lal was already a famous pathologist at that time, while his wife Vandana too had trained in pathology. Vandanaji is an ideal woman. She commanded my respect right from the beginning. Most people get annoyed with me, but she is one person who has never displayed any anger towards me.

I returned to Bharatpur with Prabhu's permission and started racking my brains on the matter at hand. Which MP should I contact? How should I begin my search? The questions were endless and the prospect was daunting. I finally decided to limit the hunt to my own state. I was from Rajasthan and there were twenty-five MPs to choose from. But whom to choose?

I didn't have too many connections in the area, because I had spent much of my teen years with Babaji. One day, while I was still mulling over the problem, I thought of my schoolmate, Jagraj Singh. I had learnt that his brother Kamal Singh was close to Rajesh Pilot, the MP from Dausa. This, then, was my solution.

I spoke to Jagraj, with whom I enjoyed family ties. He promised to have a word with his brother when he came to Bharatpur. When Kamalji eventually landed in Bharatpur, I collared him and said, 'Bhaisahib, Babaji has asked me to bring an MP to Him.'

'So, what's the big deal? Come to Delhi with Jagraj and I'll introduce you to Mr Rajesh Pilot.'

The meeting was set.

I went to Rajesh Pilot's residence in Delhi armed with an album full of Babaji's photographs. Kamalji introduced us. When I tried to show him Babaji's photographs, he demurred and said, 'Look, I stay far away from the clutches of Babas. You can meet Rama if you like.'

He introduced me to his wife Rama, and I came out of his house temporarily defeated.

Meanwhile, Babaji had come to Delhi. He was staying at Dr Rao's house in Green Park; one of His supreme devotees. Babaji affectionately addressed him as 'Sadhu Babaji'. His house was like a temple, full of lamps that were always lit. He was a Sanskrit scholar, an eminent engineer and a famous financial consultant. He was also involved in testing soil that was used for making big buildings. He has four offices in India. One of them in Delhi, while the remaining three were down south in Bangalore (now Bengaluru), Madras (now Chennai) and Secunderabad.

Dr Rao was the one who designed the blueprint of the map for the Ranikhet temple and oversaw its construction with Babaji's permission. In Haidakhan, it was he who later (after Babaji left us) had the samadhi and the gate to the cave built in the South Indian style.

Quite often, Babaji would come down from Haidakhan in Dr Rao's ambassador car, which he had nicknamed the 'Agni Rath' (fire chariot). Babaji would frequently comment on Raoji's spendthrift nature and once remarked, 'If we ever give him a lakh rupees in the morning, he'll manage to spend it by evening.'

When I learnt that Babaji was in town, I asked Kamal to fix a meeting for me with Ramaji. He took me to her. I told her, 'Ramaji, a very big saint has come to Delhi, you should come with me for darshan.'

She didn't seem very enthusiastic and said, 'Take Kamal bhai.'

I took Kamal Singh to Babaji with two other people. They spent the evening with Him. When we arrived at Dr Rao's house, Babaji was sitting on a takht and throwing fruits at His devotees. I knew His *leela*. But the others didn't and it created a bad impression.

When Kamal returned to the Pilot residence, Ramaji asked him, 'What was the Baba like?'

'He was throwing fruits at His female devotees,' was the response. *Jaise rahi bhavna jaki, Prabhu ki murat tin dekhi taisi.* (God's image exactly matches the thoughts a person has about Him). It is all a matter of faith.

The deadlock remained. I had failed once again to set up a meeting. But I did not give up.

Shortly afterwards, I found out that that Pilotji was a Hanuman devotee. I felt a glimmer of hope, because Mahant Deendayalji, the priest of the Hanuman temple in Connaught Place, Delhi, was Babaji's follower. I strategized. I called upon Ramaji and asked her to accompany me to the temple in Connaught Place. She consented. The visit was fixed for 4 p.m.

Prior to the visit, I went to the temple and prepped the Mahantji. I told him to invite Ramaji for tea to his house after the visit was over.

At 4 p.m. I escorted Kamal Singh, Ramaji and her children, Sarika and Sachin, to the temple. It is an extremely ancient temple. After the visit, mindful of my instructions, Mahantji invited us to his house. He ushered us into a room full of Babaji's photographs in myriad moods. Ramaji kept looking at them. In my mind I thought, 'Prabhu, it's now up to you to call her.'

She finally asked Mahantji, 'Who is the man in the photographs?'

'That's Haidakhan Baba. He is an avatar of Lord Shiva,' said Mahantji. 'Vijay can tell you a lot more, because he spent several years with Him.'

I started describing Babaji's various *leelas* to her. Ramaji sat in rapt attention, listening to me as I told her of Babaji's magical powers. 'It was for His darshan that I wanted to take you,' I said finally.

All this time, Mahantji had been waiting patiently while I spoke. When I fell silent, he gave us all prasad, and a short time later we left.

On the way back, Ramaji asked me where Babaji lived. 'In Haidakhan,' I told her.

She had obviously never heard of it and asked, 'Where is it?'

I told her that it was located in Nainital District. By now, she was determined to meet Babaji and repeatedly said, 'I have to go to Haidakhan.'

When Rajeshji was apprised of her intent, he informed her that he had to go to Guwahati the next day. But she was adamant, so Rajeshji cancelled his programme at Guwahati, and we all left for Haidakhan in his ambassador car at 3 p.m. on the following day. I had alerted Muniraj in advance of the Pilot family's impending arrival, and he had arranged rooms for them at Kailash View Hotel for the night. The hotel belonged to an individual who had been nicknamed Jogamal by Prabhu.

Our party of eight people reached the hotel at around 11 p.m. Rajesh and Rama Pilot had brought Sarika and Sachin with them. Kamal Singh, Gyan, and a security guard were also in tow.

The next morning, Muniraj (Trilok Singhji) came to meet them and I introduced him to Rajeshji and Ramaji. At 8 a.m. we left for Haidakhan. On the way, I told Rajeshji that Muniraj's son-in-law's sister was married to Harish Rawat, who was also an MP. He represented Ranikhet at that time.

Horses had been arranged for the trip at Jamrani dam. Rajeshji mounted a horse and took Sachin with him. He was around three years old at that time. Sarika sat on another horse with her mother. I ambled on foot beside them. It was a pleasant trek and very scenic. At places, we had to cross the river. I had walked to Haidakhan so many times that I was used to it.

When we reached, I first took Rajeshji to Hanumanji's idol for darshan, which was on the way to the ashram. Babaji was in the cave at the time and a kirtan was going on when we arrived. I went up to Babaji with Rajesh and Ramaji and they bowed to the Lord. A recitation of the *Hanuman Chalisa* was underway. Ramaji wept at Babaji's feet. He tried to calm her. After visiting the temples beside the cave, we walked towards the ashram.

Rajeshji was on a tight schedule and had planned to return immediately, but the ambience of the ashram tugged at him and he said that he wished to stay. I spoke to Babaji and asked Him if the Pilot family could stay on. Babaji replied, 'This is a place for sages and saints. Come later.'

Babaji's tenets of hospitality are worth learning. Nobody who met Him once could forget Him.

The horses had been readied by the river for the return journey. Babaji came down the stairs to see them off. Everyone was preparing to mount the horses. Babaji took a swift look at the equines and called out to Ramaji. He asked her to sit on a white horse with Sarika. Sachin was seated on his father's mount. We then bid Babaji adieu and left.

I walked beside Rajeshji and started entertaining him with stories about Babaji. Roughly two kilometres from the ashram, Rajeshji's horse suddenly stumbled and reared, tossing Sachin into the air. He fell on some stones. His father tried to grab him, but his foot got stuck in a stirrup and he tumbled to the ground.

The horse took fright and reared once again, and this time it looked as if he was going to stamp Rajeshji with his hooves. Without a thought, I leapt forward and covered his body with mine to protect him. The horse was still standing with its forelegs in the air. I shrieked. At this point, the owners of the horses rushed forward and managed to control the alarmed equine in the nick of time.

I helped Rajeshji up. He was in something of panic. 'How is my son?'

Sachin was fine; he had escaped his fall without any injuries. Rajeshji on the other hand had emerged from the incident with a few minor scratches. He had sustained them when his leg had got caught in the stirrup. Once he realized that all was well, he turned to me gratefully and said, 'Vijay, you threw yourself at me with no thought for your own safety, even though there were so many others around?'

'How could I not?' I replied. 'I was the one who brought you to Haidakhan. If something had happened to you, the stigma would have been mine, and I would not have been able to live with it.'

A new sound broke into the scene. A devotee had reached the spot to ascertain whether we were all right. 'Babaji sent me,' he panted. He had obviously run all the way down.

We all looked at each other in surprise. The ashram was two kilometres away and the accident had only taken place minutes ago. How had Babaji known? Once it had been established that there were no major injuries, the devotee went back to Haidakhan and we resumed our journey.

Ramaji eyed her husband doubtfully and asked him if he had had any negative thoughts about Babaji.

'There was nothing wrong with Him, so how could I have had any negative thoughts?' He responded.

At Haldwani, Rajeshji took a tetanus shot and we drove back to Delhi. When I met him next, he told me that the vehicle that was to take him around in Guwahati (the trip that he had cancelled last minute) had met with an accident. The driver had broken his leg, and the others in the car had also been injured.

I laughed and said, 'It's good that you did not go.' I then told him that Babaji had immeasurable powers. 'A capable guru can reduce the impact of an accident. This is what the shastras say. By going to Haidakhan, the major accident that awaited you in Guwahati was averted. Prabhu cannot wipe out your karma. But He can reduce its effect.'

By now, Rajesh and Ramaji had complete faith in Babaji's powers. Whenever Babaji came to Delhi or Vrindavan, they would visit him. They had also developed a deep fondness for me and wanted me to stay with them.

61

THE CHOPPER AFFAIR!

Every detail of 3 February 1984 is etched in my mind in black and white, in all its starkness. Babaji was pulling me to Him, and I was missing Him with a terrible ache that was almost physical. I reached Kathgodam at nine in the morning by car and began the walk to Haidakhan. The distance from Jamrani dam to Haidakhan was about six to seven kilometres. There was a bridge over the river. At some places, it was so low that one had to wade through thigh-high water. Then came the climb, on a path that ribboned the mountains.

I reached Haidakhan at about 3 p.m. and knocked on the door. Gaura, Babaji's first foreign devotee who had been so named by Him, opened it, giving me a huge smile of welcome. 'Babaji was missing you.' I almost ran to Him and bowed at His feet.

'Birju!' Exclaimed Babaji. 'We were thinking about you.' He then inquired, 'Did Modi accept the money for the helicopter ride?'

'No, Prabhu,' I said.

Babaji had flown down from Calcutta to Delhi that January. Before flying out from Calcutta, He had told me, 'Birju, we will go by helicopter from Delhi to Haidakhan. Hire one. We shall pay the fare.'

Babaji had agreed to stay at Rajesh Pilot's house during his stopover in Delhi. He had also asked me to request for a car at the landing site itself. Pilot was a member of Parliament (MP) from the Congress party. I mentioned Babaji's instructions in passing to him, and he went ahead and booked BK Modi's helicopter, inspite of Babaji's attempts to stop him. Modi was Pilotji's friend.

I then requested Mr Pilot to let me know the helicopter fare. He replied that the cost of the flight was Rs 40,000 per hour, and the helicopter would take-off from Safdarjung Airport in South Delhi. Rajesh Pilot, his wife Ramaji and both their children came to the airport with several other devotees to see Babaji off.

I must have looked anxious. Noticing this, Babaji said, 'Son, don't worry, we will pay for the helicopter.'

'I'm not worried about that,' I said, trying to appear nonchalant.

Just then, the pilot came up to us and said, 'The helicopter is ready.'

Pilot made the introductions. He first introduced Modiji to Babaji and told Him, 'This is Mr BK Modi. He owns the helicopter and will fly with you till Rampur. The other gentleman is his pilot. His name is Vijay Trehan. He will take you the rest of the way, after Modiji drops off at Rampur.'

They both bowed to Babaji. BK Modi had a factory at Rampur and had decided to join Babaji and his entourage on the chopper trip. Trehanji became quite devoted to Babaji and would later go on to become the chairman of Vayudoot (a joint-venture helicopter company) by Babaji's grace.

They all climbed into the helicopter—Babaji, Maha Muniraj, Shastriji and Bamba Devi of Bombay. BK sat in front, next to Trehanji. The chopper took off and soon disappeared into the distance. Once they were out of sight, the Pilot family and I turned to leave the airport.

Before we parted, I reminded Rajeshji about the fare. 'Babaji has instructed me to pay the fare. Please let me know where I have to make the payment.'

Rajesh Pilot followed up on the matter and had a word with Trehanji, who told him that BK Modi had refused to accept any payment for the helicopter ride. 'Tell Pilotji that just as Babaji is his guru, He has become mine too!'

want you to go to people.' Bamba Devi and the others were present at the time.

I apologized for the error of my ways and said that from now on I would do whatever He wished. The next day, He went back to Vrindavan.

By now, Rajeshji had become so fond of me that he would call me whenever he was in Bharatpur. As long as he was on tour in the area, I would be with him. I always wanted Babaji to bestow His grace on the Pilot family.

Babaji was staying at Dr Rao's house. I went there for His darshan. For some reason, Rajeshji and Ramaji could not accompany me. Babaji noticed and said, 'We scolded you. You must have told Ramaji. That's why she didn't come.'

'No, Prabhu. I did not tell her,' I replied.

That evening, I went to the Pilot residence and informed them that Babaji was in Delhi at Dr Rao's house. Rajeshji hared off to meet Babaji the same evening and requested Him to grace his house. The following day, Babaji went there for a short while in the evening and left as soon as the *aarti* and puja were over.

On several occasions, Rajeshji would prod me to go to Babaji with a question that was constantly running through his mind, 'Ask Babaji when I'll become a minister.'

I asked Babaji. He said, 'Let the time come, we will definitely tell you.'

On another occasion, Babaji was at Sabharwalji's house in Tilak Nagar in Delhi. I informed Rajeshji that Babaji was in Delhi. 'We should go there.'

We drove to Delhi through the night by jeep. Ratan Singh, Executive Engineer at the Waterworks, was with us. He became an MP from Bharatpur after retirement.

We reached Sabharwalji's house after a bath, at 4.30 in the morning. Rajeshji, Ramaji and their children loved to get *chandan* paste applied by Babaji, which He would do with his own hands. Rajeshji liked to stand in line, but the queue was very long. Now and then, Babaji would call out to devotees. He spotted Rajeshji and summoned him. We went in and emerged with *chandan* on our brows. Babaji asked Rajeshji to stay back in the room and wait. The rest of us went out. After the *chandan* had been applied on everyone, He called me in. Sabharwalji and Shastriji were sitting in the room with some other devotees. Rajeshji, as I mentioned earlier, was already there.

Babaji said, 'Rajeshji, we can make you a minister, but only if you raise your voice against corruption.'

Rajeshji replied, 'What can I do on my own?'

Babaji's response was: 'Why do you consider yourself weak? Lord Rama was alone, Krishna was alone, but they changed everything. You should have courage.'

Babaji then turned to me. 'Birju, we will dictate. You write.'

A letter was addressed to Mrs Indira Gandhi, and its gist was as follows: 'Mr Giani Zail Singh is not auspicious for the Congress. When he was home minister, he had weapons transported to the Golden Temple.' He made me close the letter with the words, 'We can save this world. Signed – 1008 Haidakhan Baba.'

Once the letter was composed, He said, 'Rajeshji, hand this letter to Indira Gandhi.'

Inside, in Babaji's presence, Rajeshji quietly took the letter, but as soon as we came out, he said, 'Vijay, you keep this. Giani Zail Singhji is my friend. I will not be able to give this letter to Indira Gandhi.'

That evening, Babaji asked, 'Will Rajeshji be able to deliver the letter? No, he will not. This is a task that requires courage.'

'He gave the letter to me as soon as we went out,' I told Him and recounted what Rajeshji had said to me.

Babaji said wryly, 'We knew.'

The wheel of time moved on. Babaji was coming to Delhi from Calcutta, and this time He had agreed to stay with Rajesh Pilot. He called me from Calcutta and said, 'Wherever our plane lands, get a car to pick us up with Rajeshji. Private cars are not allowed into the airport.'

Shastriji and Muniraj had accompanied Babaji. They all came to 3, Safdarjung Road, where Babaji had consented to stay for a day. The next day, a helicopter was supposed to take them to Haidakhan. I have mentioned this earlier.* While eating prasad that night, Rajeshji and Ramaji said, 'Babaji, please tell Vijay to stay with us.'

He said, 'No.'

The next day, as He climbed into the helicopter, He said, 'Son, Ramaji and Rajeshji are very insistent. Why don't you stay with them?' And He flew off to Haidakhan.

Rajeshji said, 'Vijay, now that we have Babaji's permission, you must stay with us.'

The second phase of my life began. I turned from religion to politics.

---

* See chapter 61 'The Chopper Affair!'

63

BABAJI TRIES TO MARRY ME OFF

I was stunned when I heard that Modiji had refused to accept payment for the chopper ride. When I met up with Babaji at Haidakhan, I apprised Him of the situation.

Babaji was philosophical and said, 'Modiji could not ask for money.'

Dismissing the matter, Babaji then said, 'Birju, come and give us a bath.'

Both Gaura and I attended to His ablutions in the bathroom near the Sheeshmahal. Babaji said, 'Birju, believe in the shelter of our feet, water them.'

I started pouring water over His feet.

'We are everything,' He continued. 'Believe in us.'

I said, 'Prabhu, I do believe in you. You are everything to me.'

'No, we are not!' He countered, disbelievingly.

Gaura laughed. But I took Babaji's words to heart. He was transcendent. The fact of the matter was that of late I had left Babaji's shelter and had been spending more time with Mr Rajesh Pilot, who was a politician from my constituency. I had started becoming blinded by power and had left the path of truth and taken off on the road to evil. But I could not admit to the truth before Him.

Gaura and I dressed Babaji. As soon as He was ready, Babaji gave me two pieces of cloth to have them stitched into a pair of trousers and shirt. He also handed me some money to meet their tailoring cost. It was for Muniraj's son's wedding. I kept trying to refuse, but He ignored my protestations and thrust the said items on me. I asked Him whether He would make it to the wedding or not. He said very gently that He would try.

There was a short silence, and then He told me, 'Birju, we have only one worry now. We should get you married.'

'In December, I will consider it. But not now,' I responded, firmly.

'No, we want to get you married now,' He said and took my hand, dragging me towards the temple where many foreign devotees attired in black clothes were sitting.

Why are they in black clothes? I wondered. Most of them had shaved heads.

He held my hand and marched me to His foreign and native devotees and announced, 'Is there a good bride for this boy?'

It is true that Babaji was joking, but His declaration made me very nervous. Babaji was oblivious to my discomfort, and His words were greeted with gales of laughter and a thunderous round of applause.

Deeply embarrassed, I said, 'Bhagwan, why are you making fun of me?'

As usual, He did not reply. Instead, He took me out and we sat near the Peepal tree. After the kirtan that night, Babaji retreated to His hut and the rest of us also turned in.

The next morning, we waited for Babaji outside His hut to have *chandan* applied by Him. This done, everyone got busy in their daily chores while Babaji sat beneath the Peepal tree and performed a havan that lasted for about half an hour. Only two or three devotees were allowed to attend it, and I was one of them. He then sat in meditation and, at around eight in the morning, He went to the temple where His *aarti* was performed. After that, all of us went down to the river with Him, where He put everyone to work.

His devotees began collecting boulders from the Gautami Ganga, which would be used to build a wall. All His foreign devotees were still in black clothes. I again wondered why. I tried to join them in their assigned task, but Babaji stopped me. 'No, Birju, you will not go. You have done enough such work in the past.'

At noon, He called a halt and everyone was allowed to go back to the ashram.

He retreated to His hut. In the evening, Babaji joined the devotees at the Gautami Ganga. Sitting near a *dhuni* at the river bank, He said, 'Birju, shave your head, we will free you from this world.'

I was not amenable and said, 'No, I have shaved my head several times before. I will not do it now.' In the face of my obstinacy, He told me to give some strands of my hair as an offering to Him. I yielded and went to the barber, who was sitting nearby and told him, 'Motiji, cut some hair.'

After the haircut, I washed my head in the Ganges and came back to Babaji. He started nagging me to get married once again. 'Birju, we want to get you married.'

I reiterated that I was not ready to get married at that point of time and that I would rather wait till December. He then called Pratap Singh, the headman of Kusum Kheda, a village near Haldwani, and told him to find a bride for me because He wanted to see me married. The next day, He left for Haldwani. This made me extremely nervous. God knows whom He would marry me to! He had become quite obstinate about it. I started thinking of going home. The next day, Pratap Singh left.

I knew Babaji was the living God, and yet I refused to abide by several orders that He issued to me. I am atoning for those lapses to this day.

On 6 February, I told Babaji, 'I am going home now.'

'You will not go,' He said.

But I put my foot down and refused to back off. I was petrified that Babaji would wed me to some strange girl. My heart was pulling me away. I changed my clothes and went back to Him.

He noticed my change of attire and said, 'If you are going, then it is your decision.'

I tried to reassure Him. 'I'll come back soon.'

'Who knows what will happen,' He remarked and reluctantly gave me permission to leave. His eyes remained glued on me till I got into the truck.

I left with a heavy heart. I did not really want to leave Him, but the fear that He would force me to wed drove me away. Yet, even then, strange questions kept running through my mind: why had Babaji asked everyone to dress in black? Why was the Ramdhun, from the *Ramayana*, playing at Haidakhan instead of '*Om Namah Shivay*'? Why was everyone being asked to shave their heads? Why were devotees doing tarpan (libation) in the river? All these things were making me uneasy. I was filled with a dreadful apprehension, because they were all part of the death rituals.

A few days later, Rajesh Pilot came to Bharatpur. He said, 'Vijay, will you come with me to Gopalgarh (his constituency) tomorrow?' Shiv Charan Mathur, the then chief minister of Rajasthan, was to lay the foundation stone for the construction of some deep wells there.

64

BABAJI TAKES SAMADHI

It was 14 February 1984. We were returning from the programme at Gopalgarh when Ramaji's message reached Pilot sahib. 'Tell Vijay that Babaji has taken samadhi.'

Extremely distressed, he broke the news to me very gently. I felt the ground beneath me shift. I panicked and took off for Delhi immediately. I kept trying to reassure myself that Babaji would be fine. Hadn't I witnessed Him leaving His body several times in the past? But a deep dread had settled in my heart.

I reached Delhi at 4 a.m. and caught the 5 a.m. bus from there. I arrived at Kathgodam at about 1 p.m. and started walking to Haidakhan. I saw several buses and trucks returning. I knew then that something untoward had happened. I broke down.

When I reached Haidakhan that evening, I learnt that Babaji had taken samadhi and they had already buried Him. I went to His tomb and wept.

Muniraj said, 'Birju, we waited for a long time for you.'

'It was my misfortune that I did not have the privilege of seeing His mortal remains,' I told him sombrely.

Naveenji gave me a rudraksha necklace (a seed traditionally used for prayer beads in Hinduism. Rudraksha beads are highly revered as the tears of Shiva and are said to connect the wearer-seeker directly to the source of existence and to pure consciousness) and two small towels and said, 'We kept them at Babaji's feet throughout the night. They still smell of *chandan*.'

I silently accepted the necklace and towels and touched them to my forehead before packing them away carefully with the rest of my belongings. I still have them with me to this day.

I finally mustered up courage and asked him what had happened. Muniraj told me that Babaji was in His hut. When He did not appear for morning kirtan, some devotees knocked at His door. But there was no response. When there was still no response from inside even in the afternoon, they broke open the door and went in. They found Him unconscious on His *aasan*. Frightened, they called a doctor from Haldwani. The doctor examined Lord Haidakhan and announced, 'Babaji is no more.'

Today, I wonder why he had not stopped me when I wanted to leave. Were those black clothes and shaven heads an advance message from Him of His impending departure? Was He deliberately trying to drive me away with His talk of marriage and His insistence that I shave my head, because He thought I would not be able to bear being witness to His final journey?

My mind often goes back to another strange incident that had taken place at Dr VVS Rao's house at Green Park in Delhi, not very long before Babaji left His body. Babaji was sitting on a swing at Raoji's residence while a kirtan was being performed. Shastriji was standing beside Him. He called me and my friend, Vijay Bhatiani, and asked us to sing a farewell song for Him. Shastriji said, '*Lo vidai, lo vidai, lo vidai* (Take farewell, take farewell, take farewell).'

At that time, on the surface it had appeared as if Shastriji was admonishing us for chasing worldly goods in a material world instead of absorbing Babaji's teachings and focusing on our spiritual growth. But now, having gone over it, I think that He was making Shastriji tell us that 'you have come here and neither recognized us nor learnt anything from us.'

Babaji too had made a statement that had appeared abstruse at the time, but in effect, practically meant the same thing. He had said, '*Naukri laga di hai, 4 rupai 8 chapati* (We have got you a job of four rupees and eight chapatis). *Bhagwan jaa rahe hain* (God is leaving). *Tum ne yahan humse kuch bhi nahin sikha* (You have learnt nothing from us).'

Vijay Bhatiani and I had bowed hastily before Him and had retreated from His wrath at the time. The devotees present had also not made too much of the incident. They thought, 'Prabhu has made so many ashrams, He has gathered so many Indian and foreign bhakts, where will He leave us and go?' But when was Babaji's *leela* ever so simple?

Even today, I keep trying to make sense of the incident.

Was Babaji scolding me for not following Him more strictly? Or was He telling me that He was about to leave the world? Perhaps it was a bit of both. He definitely wasn't happy with my foray into the world of politics and often warned me that I would gain nothing from it. But He knew my attachment to Him was genuine and would certainly have been aware of the depth of the emotional shake-up I would endure once I discovered that He had taken samadhi. It was possible that He was trying to tell me in a roundabout way that He was not long of this world.

He was the Lord of the Cosmos, and I so small before His infinite divinity. How could I understand His cosmic play and mysterious ways? But one thing I'm sure of—we were all off-beam when we thought that Babaji would become entrapped in our *maya jaal* (snare of illusions) and stay because of His attachment to us. How wrong we were!

Babaji's words come back to me today. 'We will be inside our room and people will be waiting for us outside. When they open the door, they will not find us there.'

He had said this in 1972, and meticulously described the scene of His death a full twelve years before He left us. It was the day Makkhanji had told me that we were all living under Babaji's *leela* and didn't always understand what He was up to or what He was trying to tell us.

65

IN THE HURLY BURLY

Truth is the first casualty in politics. Babaji had ended His *leela* and left His body. It was a strange time. Whereas at one time, when I was with Babaji I used to speak the truth from morning to night, here in the world of politics, I told lies all the time. In politics, people seldom tell the truth.

My mother was worried about my single state. My sister was already married, and this had left her very lonely. One day, my niece Guddu's husband Madanji brought Pyare Lal Guptaji to meet me. He traded in sanitary fittings at Chawri Bazar in Delhi and was a simple and very straightforward soul.

'I have come to see you for my daughter's hand in marriage,' he announced without beating about the bush. It was on this note that I plunged into the world of matrimony.

I went with my friend Vijay Bhatiani to see Neeru in Chawri Bazaar and took a shine to her immediately. I had only one request. Once we tied the knot, she would serve my mother and stay with her. Guptaji politely accepted my terms. My wife was from a wealthy home and had never travelled in anything but a car, while I was from a middle-class family.

The '*god bharai*' ceremony took place in Dr Rao's house in Vasant Vihar, where apart from my own family, my friend Vijay Bhatiani, his wife Meeraji, and all the members of the Pilot family congregated. Ramaji filled Neeru's maang (parting of the hair on the head) with vermillion with her own hands, because she considered her as her sister.

On 5 May 1986, I got married with great pomp at the Hindu Mahasabha Bhavan on Mandir Marg in Delhi. Almost all of Babaji's devotees graced the occasion. Among those in attendance were Muniraj, cine actor Shammi Kapoor and his wife Neilaji, my own family and relatives, Devi's kin, Shastriji, Rajesh Pilotji and family, and other prominent people from Bharatpur.

I'm glad that God bestowed me with a wife like Neeru. She is pious, very kind and calm by nature. She took care of my mother as long as she was alive and never hindered me, even though she didn't like me being away from home. I lived in Delhi with the Pilot family, while she stayed uncomplainingly in Bharatpur with our two children and brought them up single-handedly.

Today, both my kids are engineers. They are very smart but with a strong religious streak in them. Babaji too has never abandoned me. Whenever I ran into obstacles, I prayed to Lord Haidakhan and every hurdle vanished.

A few months after Babaji left His body, Rajesh Pilot became a minister in the Government of India. At the time, I was in Bharatpur and still unmarried. People thronged to congratulate him. But I felt a strange reluctance to go to Delhi.

Then one day I got a call and Rajeshji said, 'Vijay, everyone has come to me except you. What's the matter?'

I said, 'Bhaisahib, nothing's the matter. My tapasya (rigorous prayers to attain something) is over. You have become a minister.'

He asked me to come to Delhi. I tried to explain.

'Bhai!' I said, 'I will not be able to live in an environment where you have to lie from morning to evening. I used to speak the truth from dawn to midnight.'

He was unimpressed. 'Come to Delhi once and let's talk about it.'

Ignoring my reluctance, he rang up an IAS officer and instructed him to bring me to Delhi. Helpless in the face of Rajeshji's persistence, I reached Delhi and congratulated Rajeshji and Ramaji.

Rajeshji held all the cards and cornered me effortlessly. He said, 'Vijay, we asked Babaji if we could keep you with us. He gave us His approval. Are you going to say that you will not obey Babaji's orders?'

I was on a losing wicket, but still game. I tried my best to valiantly wiggle out of the situation. 'You know that's not true. Even if I'm not with you all the time, I'll still keep coming.'

He behaved as if he hadn't heard me and said, 'No. You are my trusted person. You will stay with me in my department. I will keep you like my brother.'

I eventually surrendered to my fate. Rajeshji was a hard man to refuse, so I joined the Ministry of Surface Transport as his PA. It set the pattern of things to come, and I went from department to department as his portfolios changed. He was happy with my dedication and hard work, and I plodded on to the best of my ability.

I spent all my time honestly but was not too happy about being away from my children. I was also worried about getting permanent work. One day, I made an announcement at 10 Akbar Road. I told Rajeshji and his wife that I wanted to go back to Bharatpur and live with my family.

He said, 'Look, Vijay, I am thinking of fixing permanent employment for you. You have to work for me, whether you do it happily or unhappily.'

He compelled me and I continued to live on his assurances. But God had something else in store for me. Also, at the back of my mind, Babaji's words continued to haunt me. He had warned me that I would gain nothing from the political world.

One day, Pilot sahib and I travelled to Bandikui by Pooja Express, as he had to participate in some religious programmes in the surrounding villages. While we were in the train, he kept saying, 'I will settle things for you on Monday. I promised I'll look after you and I will.'

He must have said this to me at least thrice.

'You can do it at your ease, Bhaisahib,' I responded. 'Why are you getting so anxious?'

We got off at Bandikui and started attending the various events that had been lined up for him. On the way back, he said, 'You come to Delhi by the Pooja Express, I'll take a flight from Jaipur. I would have taken you there with me, but I know you'll insist on staying back once we're there.'

We were sitting in the new Mahindra Marshall, a seven-seater that had just been introduced into the market. I always used to sit behind him so that I could jot things down; one never knew when he would come up with some instructions. Besides, I wasn't much of a conversationalist.

We parted at Bandikui. 'Go to Delhi by train, Vijay. I'll see you there.'

It was the last time I saw him.

I hopped onto the Pooja Express at Bandikui whilst he carried on to Jaipur. He never made it there, as he met his end in a headlong collision with a bus in his constituency at Dausa. Ram Singh, the constable who had taken my seat in the Mahindra, was also killed.

As news of the accident spread, my family took fright. They thought that I had been in the vehicle at the time of the accident.

After his death, his daughter Sarika met me in Delhi at their residence. Her marriage was only a few months old. 'You won't leave us, will you?' She said, as she handed me a letter from an Australian astrologer Barbara, who had been Babaji's devotee. The letter in a nutshell told me to stay on with the Pilot family as it was the only way that 'Rajeshji will find peace'.

Ramaji became MP from Dausa after Rajeshji's death. She had earlier fought an election from Bansur for a seat in the Legislative Assembly, which she had lost. It had hurt Rajeshji's reputation at that time, causing him deep concern.

When Sachin was old enough, he took over the Dausa seat from his mother. After he won the elections, I addressed a letter to him and left it with Ram Dev, who used to make tea in their house for visitors from the constituency, and left for Bharatpur. In the letter, I wrote, 'Sachinji, you have become a Member of Parliament. You are in a good situation today. I have held you in my lap and will not be able to call you Sir. Keep good people about you. I pray for a bright future for you.'

Two days later, I received a phone call from him. 'At least come and meet me once.'

I went.

'You've served my parents for so many years,' said Sachin when I met him. 'Don't leave me. I will undertake the responsibility for your whole family. I will certainly do something for you. How can you leave me at such a time?'

How could I leave? His words were compelling, and I stayed on.

However, the onset of power brought about inevitable changes in his behaviour, and my desire to leave turned increasingly intense. Then Babaji's grace came to my rescue, and Dausa became a reserved constituency. Sachin could no longer contest from there, he had to shift to a new seat.

Finding the opening that I had been seeking, I grabbed my chance and went to Sachinji. I asked him to release me. 'I knew the people of Dausa. I will be of no use to you in a different constituency.'

Sachinji let me go. After serving the Pilot family for twenty-five years, I was finally free.

What Babaji had once said had come true. I reaped no rewards from the world of politics. I went back home to my family in Bharatpur, where my journey had begun all those years ago. Life had come full circle.

66

FOREIGN TRIP

Babaji never went abroad. He always called foreign devotees to Haidakhan and a number of them just stayed on. Most sadhus start making foreign trips as soon as they become famous, but there are some like Babaji who remain the same. Babaji sent Muniraj abroad as His representative at the request of His foreign devotees, along with Dr VVS Rao, the general secretary of the trust that He had formed. Amar Singh Chacha was the treasurer. After Babaji left His body, Maha Muniraj took me abroad on 3 September 1992.

It was a forty-five-day trip. Maha Muniraj was accompanied by Shastriji, Dr Arvind Lal, and Shastriji's son, Chandradev. We visited several countries during this trip, chief among them being Switzerland, France, Austria, Germany, Italy and Holland, where beautiful temples and ashrams of Lord Haidakhan had been built. Chants of '*Om Namah Shivay*' resounded everywhere.

Maha Muniraj introduced me as the foremost devotee of Haidakhan Baba. I used to speak in Hindi, and Dr Arvindji would translate what I said into English. Dr Lal always gave me a lot of affection like he would to a brother. He also arranged the different visas that were required for the trip through his embassy and other bureaucratic connections. A joint secretary in the petroleum ministry also helped. Palluben and her husband, Yogendra Bhai, from Mumbai also came to Cisternino, Italy during the trip.

Shastriji gave discourses, and both he and Maha Muniraj responded to the questions put forth by devotees.

EPILOGUE

Troubles came and went, but I survived. I had stayed in close touch with Babaji for fourteen years. I saw His *leela*, and even after He left His body, I continued to go to Haidakhan and Ranikhet for Navratri each year and to Vrindavan for the Prakatya Utsav. His Grace over me was endless, and it helped me weather each storm that came my way. Not for a minute did I feel that He had abandoned me.

Maha Muniraj (Trilok Singhji) took over the ashram after Babaji took samadhi. He became the chairman of the Haidakhan trust. As Babaji's successor, he steered the ashram smoothly and with immense grace; his affection for me remained unwavering and somehow, he made Babaji's loss bearable for me. When he went on foreign trips, he dragged me along and asked me to preach Babaji's teachings. He also asked me to add new devotees. New entrants into our fold were treated with enormous respect. The ashram grew over the years and the ranks of Babaji's devotees continued to swell. Even today, His disciples feel the immortal fragrance of Babaji's presence continuously.

Foreign devotees who embraced Babaji's philosophies wholeheartedly still come to the ashram. His first such devotee was Gaura. The other prominent names who still come to Haidakhan are Khadkuji, Pujariji, Raghuveerji, Gangaji, Sabinaji, Shivaniji, Moti Maa, Hargovindji, Loknathji, and Pratibhaji. Hargovindji is very gentle and performs all his tasks with great enthusiasm to this day.

After Maha Muniraj's passing, there was a void, because he left this world without nominating a successor. But he had formed a committee to run the ashram, comprising Mr Alok Banerjee, Sandeep Tandon, Murali Shukla and I. Later, all the devotees—Indian and foreign—unanimously elected Alokji as President of Haidakhan Society. He was a man of simple tastes who watched over everything and everyone with an impartial eye. His tenure was excellent. His colleague Mr Sanjeev Sarna, the general secretary of the society, was also wonderful. He helped in every way and put in a great deal of effort to ensure that the ashram operated smoothly.

All Haidakhandi devotees, both within the country and abroad, praise his work.

A year before Muniraj left his body, I made a prophecy at the Ranikhet temple at his behest. It was translated into English by Mr Uday Chatterjee, who was vice-chairman of the society at the time.

I declared that Babaji had been revealed by Muniraj to me; He could come anytime. All of us should devote ourselves to bhajans and kirtans and follow the canons of truth, simplicity and love. We should love everyone and refrain from demeaning each other. Babaji would only appear before us when these feelings prevailed in all of us. This prediction was assiduously propagated everywhere, both in India and abroad.

This came to pass, because one day when I had gone to Maha Muniraj to clear my doubts, I asked him, 'When will Babaji come?'

'He is here,' said Maha Muniraj. 'I have seen Him coming and going all the time. I believe that He will appear to you only when you call Him with your whole heart.'

I often used to think that I should propagate Babaji's philosophy to as many people as possible. It was in this context that I would invite people and keep asking them to attend havans at Haidakhan and Ranikhet to see Babaji's temple, so that they could prosper.

Several prominent people have visited the ashram. Among them are the Chief Minister of Rajasthan Ashok Gehlot (then Congress Working Committee member) and his family, All India Congress Committee secretary Vivek Bansal, who is in charge of Rajasthan, and journalist Ajit Mandola and his personal staff. Likewise, MP Kirori Lal Meena, retired High Court Judge Raghuvendra Singh Rathore, former Rajathan Government Health Minister Raghu Sharma, Minister of Women and Child Development Mamata Bhupesh (who was then an MLA), and Shri Rajendra Yadav, a former minister, who had darshan of Babaji earlier felt a lot of peace and solace after visiting the Ashram.

Both IAS and IPS officers also come in droves to visit Haidakhan. Former Home Secretary Pradeep Sen, Rajasthan MLA Omprakash Hundla, Mr Suresh Gupta IAS, and Mr Praveen Gupta IAS have always helped out in times of need, and thanks to them I have never suffered for want of anything. I am also grateful to Panwar sahib and his family and wish them a happy life.

In 2009, I went to Shri Lal Chandra Kataria, an MP from Jaipur Rural and now Agriculture Minister in Rajasthan, to invite him to visit the Ranikhet Temple. He said, 'I will definitely come.' I also called Mr Rajendra Singh Yadav, who was then President of the Jaipur District Congress Committee, and told him that we had to go to the Haidakhan Baba temple at Ranikhet.

Yadavji previously lived in Kichcha, as he has a flour mill there. He is a relative of Amar Singh Chacha. On Ashtami day, Lal Chand and some of his friends, along with Rajendra Yadav, reached the

Ranikhet ashram. They visited the temple and participated in the havan. On behalf of the society, I honoured them with a shawl and a thick bracelet bearing the engraving '*Om Namah Shivay*'. Thereafter, they returned to Delhi and we all became busy in our own lives.

I once requested him to help us get a telephone tower to Haidakhan. He immediately agreed and went with me to Mr Kapil Sibal, who was then Minister of Communication. The telephone tower was approved.

On another occasion, I wrote a letter to Mr Harish Rawat to repair the road to Haidakhan as it was damaged. He was Chief Minister at the time and speedily sanctioned the funds, and the road was quickly repaired. Thereafter, he started visiting Haidakhan and Ranikhet during Navratri each year. Sometimes he landed there even when there was no occasion. He told me that he finds the place very peaceful.

Mr Lal Chand Kataria is the Minister of Agriculture in the Government of Rajasthan today. He is a very gentle soul with a remarkable lack of arrogance. He enjoys Babaji's grace, and it is my belief that he will grow a lot in the future.

In 2019, Alokji's health was not too good, and he wanted to be relieved from the post of the chairman of the society. He expressed this in the Ranikhet meet, and in December 2019, he pleaded before devotees that he was not well and asked them to allow him to step down. He handed over the post of chairman to Padma Shri (Honorary) Brigadier Dr Arvind Lal, who was the vice-chairman of the society.

All the devotees, Indian and foreign, welcomed the move. Arvindji is the Chairman of Haidakhandi Society today. He is a fearless and efficient administrator. I am confident that under his guidance, the society will grow every day.

Om Namah Shivay

APPENDIX I

Global Ashrams of Haidakhan Babaji

INDIA

1. Haidakhan Vishwa Mahadham
P.O. Haidakhan
District Nainital
Uttarakhand - 263 126
Phone: +91 89580 52917, +91 93583 73452
Email: info@haidakhanbabaji.com
Website: www.haidakhandisamaj.org

2. Ananda Puri Ashram
Col B.S. Rana
Chiliyanaula, Ranikhet
District Almora
Uttarakhand- 263647
Phone +91 5662-20658
Mobile: +91 94589 65380
Email: anandpuri.ashram@gmail.com
Website: www.haidakhandisamaj.org; www.anandpuri.com

3. Bhagwan Shri 1008 Haidakhandi Go-Seva Ashram
Palluben (Pallavi Madhavlal)
Manda/Nagam
Taluka Umergam
Dist. Valsad
Gujarat- 396 156
Phone: +91 98206 24793, +91 97691 30843
Email: pallumadhavlal@yahoo.co.in

4. Samba Sada Shiva Kunj
Shiv Ram Sharma
Gopi Nath Bazaar
Vrindavan
UP - 281 121
Phone: +91 9873825708

5. Baba Haidakhan ashram
Capt B.N. Yadav
Village & Post Office: Thathwari
Tehsil: Khetri
District: Jhunjhunu
Rajasthan- 332746
Mobile: +91 88001 00112
Email: captbnyadav@gmail.com

6. Haidakhandi Samaj
Col B.S. Rana
Reg. Office: Yaday Bhawan, Malla Gorakhpur
Distt. Nainital
Uttarakhand– 263139
Phone: +91-5946 281081
Fax: +91-5946 281081

Mobile: +91 94589 65380
Email: haidakhandisamajcom@yahoo.com
Website: Haidakhandisamaj.org

GERMANY

Bhole Baba Ashram
Nadja Michel; Nirmala
Rieferath, Kalkstück 11
D-51570 Windeck-Rieferath
Phone: +49 2243 6603
Telefax: +49 2243 911 623
Email: vorstand@babajiashram.de; nadja_michel@web.de
Website: www.babajiashram.de

ITALY

1. Fondazione Bhole Baba
Fabio Pacini (Ram Lota)
Contrada Portarino 10
72014 Cisternino (BR) C.P. 138
Phone +39 080 4448735
Email: ramlota@tin.net
Website: www.bholebaba.orghttp://samajitaliano.org

2. Centro Spirituale di Pace Haidakhandi
Manjit; Dr Settimo Catalano (Tulsa Singh)
Monte Gaudio, 1 Villa San Secondo
14020 Asti
Phone: +39 0141 905393
Telefax: +39 0141 905393
Email: info@csph.net; settimo.catalana@fastwebnet.it
Website: www.csph.net

3. Haidakhandi Samaj Love Centre
Pietralunga (PG)
Villarosa – Loc.Corniole
06026 Pietralunga (PG)
Phone +39 075 933074
Email: evan.aliana@libero.it; info@babajicenter.net
Website: http://www.babajicenter.net/

SWITZERLAND

Zentrum der Einheit Schweibenalp
CH-3855 Brienz
Phone: +41 339 512 001
Email: info@schweibenalp.ch
Website: www.schweibenalp.chwww.haidakhandi-sangha.ch

THE NETHERLANDS

Sada Shiva Dham
Vrijenbergweg 60 – 62
7371 AB Loenen (Veluwe)
Phone: +31 55 505 2871
Email: sadashivadham@gmail.com
Website: http://www.babaji.nl/

USA

Haidakhandi Universal Ashram
Ramloti
P.O. Box 9 (mailing address only)
2349 Camino Baca Grande #9 (physical address but no mail delivery)

Crestone, Colorado 81131
Phone: 719 256 4108
Mobile: 719 480 5514
Email: info@babajiashram.org
Website: www.babajiashram.org

Global Centres of Haidakhan Babaji

AUSTRALIA

1. Madeleine Chaleyer, Secretary of Samaj
Email: babajiaustralia@gmail.com
Australian Facebook address: Babaji Samaj Australia

2. Jayanti Woods
PO Box 848
Nerang, Gold Coast
QLD – 4211
Phone: +61 415 382272
Email: jayanti108@usa.net

3. Kanta Dwyer
1/290 Alison Rd
Cogee, NSW – 2034
Phone: +61 296 648714
Email: kerrykantadwyer@gmail.com
3. Andrew and Kalavati Stevens
2, The Bartizan
Castlecrag, NSW
Phone: +61 299 585890
Email: aj.stevens@bigpond.com

4. Janaki & Narayan Kozeluh
17 Partridge Crt
Alice Springs, NT - 0870
Phone: +61 889 530591
Email: kozmob@internode.net.au

5. Shri Maha Deva Dham
Nan-Singh & Bhuri
22 Russell Lane
Via Bega, Kalaru, NSW- 2550
Phone: +61 264 944624
Email: nansingh@hotmail.com

6. Tiger-Singh & Deepa Amanpuri
Tathra Rd
Via Bega, Kalaru, NSW- 2550
Phone: +61 264 941829
Email: ddfunston@gmail.com

AUSTRIA

Babaji Haus Graz
Anamika Ilse Falk
Riesstrasse 238
A-8047 Graz
Phone: +43-316-301 960
Email: anamikabab@hotmail.com
Website: www.babaji-haus-graz.net

BELGIUM

Antwerp Babaji Centre
Pervijzestraat 27
B-2600 Berchem

BULGARIA

1. J.K. Krasno Selo
Mimi Koleva
Bl. 198 Ap. 4
BG-Sofia 1618
Phone: +35 9-2-566744
Email: mkoleva@aster.net

2. Dattatreya Ecological Centre
Dimitar Mavrov
Ekodar - Ltd.
P.O. Box 29
BG – Sofia 1125

CROATIA

1. Haidakhandi Love Centre,
Parvati, President
Ram Narayenne (Robert), Mahendri
Osijek, Croatia
Dubrovacka 90
31000 Osijek
Phone: +38 598 9371605
Email: kontakt@babajihrvatska.org
Website: www.babajihrvatska.org

2. Duzice 1

Visnu Datt (Vanja Cigler)
10000 Zagreb
Email: vanjacigler@yahoo.com
Web-site: www.haidakhan.net

CZECH REPUBLIC

Vera Koudelkova
Detska 128/9
CZ – 10000 Praha
Phone: +42 7813114

ESTONIA

Haidakhandi Shiva Dham
Merike Taza, Ave Oit, President
Lilleoru talu, Aruvalla küla, Rae vald
75320 Harjumaa
Phone: +372 56 499 199
Email: merike@lilleoru.ee; ave.oit@lilleoru.ee
Website: http://www.lileoru.ee

FRANCE

Le Samaj
33 rue Emile Zola
13650 Meyrargues
Phone: +33 442575961
Email: info@babaji.fr
Website: www.babaji.fr

GERMANY

1. Lazwanti, Lydia
Alamannenstr. 28
88499 Aldheim
Phone: +49 7371 927282
Fax: +49 7371 927281

2. Shri Haidakhandi Sadhana Centre
Nabburger Str. 6
92540 Altendorf
Phone: + 49 9675-234
Email: madhulm@web.de

3. Haidakhandi Spiritual Unity Centre
Elisabeth Frey
Lutonerstrasse 30
D-13581
Berlin
Phone: +49 30331 3776

4. Source of Healing Centre and Seminar House
Renata Caddy (Nila)
Alpenblick 7
D-88718 Daisendorf-Meersburg
Phone: +49 7532 6171
Fax: +49 7532 6718
Email: renata.caddy@gmx.de

5. Peter Nückel (Kushal Singh)
Robert-Mayer-Weg 2B
40591 Düsseldorf
Phone: +49 211 1705203
Email: kushal@hotmail.de

6. Elfi Wischnewski
Dürener Str. 35
40223 Düsseldorf
Phone: +49 211 5830405

7. Shyam Lal, Basanti
Radeberger Str. 14
01328 Dresden
Phone: +49 351 8115798
+49 173 3801381
Website: www.bhole-baba-dresden.de; www.touch-your-soul.de

8. Kundan Singh
Weihenstra 2/1
72800 Eningen/Achalm
Phone: +49 7121 83451

9. Kalavati
Freiburg im Breisgau
Phone: +49 761 7679499
Email: carolinerosengarth@gmx.de

10. Hans Spehr (Param Hans)
Böhlaustr 1, Hannover
Phone: +49 511-582008

11. Dr Ludwing Kalk
Burgwedeler Str. 31
30657 Hannover
Phone: +49 511 652723

12. Satyanand, Asha
Dasselstr. 24
50674 Köln
Phone/Fax: +49 221 2409669

13. Hamsa u. Shakti Schilling
Plauener Str. 2
80992 München
Phone: +49 89 1407216

14. Binsenstraße 31
48529 Nordhorn
Phone: +49 5921- 721214

15. Krishna Kumar
Höfen 16
87534 Oberstaufen
Phone: +49 8386 991351
Mobile: +49 177 9252667
Website: www.karlzauner.de

16. Manjula, Ganga Ram
Dr Matzke Str. 8
89284 Pfaffenhofen
Phone: +49 7302 920447
Email: moniseel@excite.com

17. Govinda Schlegel
Waldrach City
Phone: +49 6500 917777
Email: go@indienserver.de

18. Gertraud, Roland Reichel (Om Shanti, Ganga Singh)
Reifenberg 85
D-91365 Weilersbach
Phone: +49 9194 8985
Mobile: +49 177 56 43 451
Fax: +49 9194 4262
Email: rr@solarmobil.net
Website: www.solarmobil.net; www.reichel-verlag.de

19. Klaswipper 30
51688 Wipperfürt
Email: heikestrombach@yahoo.com

GREECE

Eleftheriadis Miltiadis (Atmaram)
Athens
Email: ematmaram@yahoo.gr
Website: www.Babaji.gr

INDIA

1. Shiv Mandir
79, K. K. Bhatta Road
Chenikuthi
Guwahati - 781003
Assam

2. Shree Haidakhandi Foundation
12/A, Amin Society
Near Usmanpura Railway Crossing
P.O. Navjivan, Naranpura
Ahmedabad – 380 013
Gujarat

3. Shree Haidakhandi Baba Mandir
Dariapur, Hilsa
Dist. Nalanda
Bihar

4. Haidakhan Lila Kshetra Dham
P.O. Nagar Khan, Village: Dhanyan
Dist. Almora, Uttarakhand

5. Shree Kurmanchal Kailash Trust
Kayavaroham
Dist. Vadodara
Gujarat- 391220

6. Shree Haidakhan Baba Mandir
Kota
Rajasthan

7. Shree Ratneshwar Mahadev
Baldev Road
Lohban
Mathura, U.P.

8. Shree Haidakhan Baba Mandir
Mandiri, Patna
Bihar

9. Madhuban Ashram
P.O. Moholi
Mathura
U.P.

10. Haidakhan Mandir
Tatipura , Murar
Gwalior, Rajasthan

11. Janakpuri Ashram
A-2/228, Janakpuri
New Delhi- 110 058
Phone: +91 99101 52350

12. Siddhashram
Near Almora, Uttarakhand

13. Kausani Ashram
Near Almora, Uttarakhand

INDONESIA

1. Haidakhandi Peace Centre
Bheru Baba (I Gede Gatot Binawa Rata)
Jalan Diponegoro No. 142A Denpasar
Bali – 80114
Phone: +62 361 235797
Mobile: +62 8124 632388
Email: bhinawa_raat@yahoo.com

2. Haidakhandi Ashram, Pondok Lamer
Pujungan
Pupuan, Tabanan
Bali- 82163

3. Baba Haidakhan Centre
Parvati
Jalan Padang Tawang I no. 99 Babakan, Canggu
Phone: +62 8987 9690 97
Email: luhmang@yahoo.com

IRELAND

Haidakhan Bhole Baba Centre
Milmorane, Ballingeary Co
Cork
Phone: +353 26 47230
Email: babajiireland@yahoo.ie

ITALY

1. Padam Singh
Haidakhandi Samaj Croce Mandir Cava Di Tirreni (SA)
Via M. Di Florio-Villa
84013 Cava Di Tirreni (SA)
Email: padam@crochemandir.net
Website: http://samajitaliano.org

2. Croce Mandir
Via M. di Florio-Villa
I – 84013 Cava dei Tirreni (SA)
Maria Grazia

Phone: +39 348 5638969
Email: info@j-amba.it
Website: www.j-amba.it/

3. Jñana Ashram
Santa Maria di Pagialla
06026 Pietralunga (PG)
Phone: +39 075 9460001

4. Sardinia Centro Hanuman
Lalla Meregaglia
Localita Baddarana
07020 Telti (O/T)
Phone: +39 0789 43599
Mobile: +39 3396 786669
Website: www.centrohanuman.com
info@centrohanuman.com- ramsevi@fastwebnet.it

JAPAN

Babaji Centre Japan
Dr Harada Shuzo
101-21 Hizure
Fujinocho, Kanagawaken
Phone: +81 42687 2868
Email: babaji@ktd.biglobe.ne.jp

LATVIA (Lettonia)

1. Babadzi Biedriba Latvija
Latviesu-Indiesu Kulturas Centrs
(Babaji society in Latvia, Latvian-Indian Culture Centre)

Hospitalu 29-21
Riga LV 1013
Phone: +37 1 29 122790
Email: estere@latnet.lv

2. Babaji Centre
Ajit & Uma
Gertrudes str. 5
Riga LV-1010
Phone: +37129739923; +37127030143

POLAND

1. Bhole Baba Seva Dham Ashram
Frans van de Logt (Paramananda)
Sw Jana 15
34 – 143
Lanckorona, near Krakow
Phone: +48 33 876 3514
Website: www.babaji.pl/

2. Shri Herakhandi Seva Dham Ashram
Krishna Kumar
Makolno 129
P.O. Box 32
57-250 Zloty Stok
Phone: +48 74 817 73 32
Fax: +48 506 116 643

RUSSIA

1. Omkar Shiva Dham Ashram
Rupali
Okunjewo Muromeceva
644099 Omsk Raj
Email: rupali@inbox.ru
Website: www.babaji.ru (in Russian)

2. Haidakhandi Love Centre
Armand & Sangheeta
Zaluchnoe, near Moscow
Phone: +7926 1271337
Email: zaluchnoe108@gmail.com
Website: http://vk.com/zaluchnoe108

3. Mahaprabhuji Ashram
219 Oktyabrskaya, Voronezh
St Malishevo subdivision
Email: kamalu@babaji.org.ua

SLOVENIA

1. Živa Centre
Maya Ram & Nandani
Tomacevo 27, Ljubljana
Phone: +386 31 857790
Website: www.babaji.si

2. Ruše, Pohorje
Dušan Grimšic, Smolnik
Phone: +386 41 554 688
Website: www.kpn-smolnik.si

3. Kriya Yoga Centre
Edmund
Vojkova 3
6210 Sezana
Website: www.sribabaji.org

SOUTH AFRICA

Laina Lesicnik
P. O. Box 438
Mooi River, 3300
South Africa
Phone: +2733 263 2275
Email: laina@futurenet.co.za

SOUTH KOREA

Ilsan Kyung Gi New Babaji Centre
Sukhdeva
Vak Suzeen
Deawoo City Plaza 625
Ilsan, Kyung Gi Korea
Phone: +82 11 777 0548
Email: sukhdeva@hotmail.com

SPAIN

Amba (Izascun Garmendia)
Irraitz Ausoa 63 bajo 2
Aritzaga Basserria
20720 Azkoitia (Guipuzcoa)
Phone: +34 6200 72847
Email: izascun.amba@gmail.com

SWEDEN

1. Ashram Sambasadashiva Dham
Bo Wahlström
Ortalalund 7457
760 40 Väddö
Phone:+46 176 50448; +46 70 2184838
Email: info@intuition-bw.com

2. Haidakhan Baba Centre
Nytorget 6
Stockholm 11640
Phone: +46 8 640 6179

THAILAND

Sri Sada Shiva Maha Avatar Mandir
Kharku & Raghuvir
Kamalaya Resort
Koh Samui
Email: john@kamalaya.com; raghu@babaji.nl
Phone: +66 81826 7938; +66 87817 3473

UKRAINE

Sita Ram Dhuni
Kamalu
Kotsyubinskovo St. 25 apt 23
Lugansk
Email: kamalu@babaji.org.ua

UNITED KINGDOM

Haidakhandi Samaj UK
Radha & Anand
Haccadown Longdown
EX6 7SA Exeter
Devon
Phone: +44 1392 811 108
Email: pujari@ombabaji.org.uk
Email: radheananda@bitinternet.com
Website: www.ombabaji.org.uk

USA

1. Carlsbad Haidakhan Centre
Nirmal Sharma
Carlsbad, California
Phone: +1 508 847 9135
Email: Sharman116@yahoo.com

2. Yorba Linda Babaji Centre
Chandresh Baba
Yorba Linda, California
Email: Jct1008@yahoo.com

3. Heartland Haidakhandi Centre
Melinda Staley
Columbia, Missouri
Email: Melindastaley@hotmail.com

4. Baba's House in Minneapolis
Colleen Buckman
Powderhorn Park

Minneapolis, Minnesota
Phone: +1 612 669 0794
Email: colleenbuckman@gmail.com

5. Karin Kabalah Centre
Alok Agrawal, Shirley Chambers
2531 Briarcliff Road
Atlanta, Georgia
Phone: +1 404 320 1038
Email: kabalah@mindspring.com

6. Houston Babaji Centre
Alexandra Kachmarik
Houston, TX 77082
Phone: +1 832 462 4869

7. Treasure Island Babaji Centre
Sharda & Jeffery Collard
Treasure Island, Florida
Phone: +1 727 363 0800

8. Jupiter Babaji Centre
Elaine Heroux
Jupiter, Florida
Phone: +1 561 398 2711
Email: elainemheroux@gmail.com

9. Delray Beach Babaji Centre
Sal & Serena Moreno
Delray Beach, Florida
Phone: +1 561 715 7967

APPENDIX II

Haidakhandi Samaj Office-Bearers and Executive Committee Members

(Hony) Brig. Dr. Arvind Lal	Chairman
Dr. Prem Chand	Vice-Chairman
Shri Uday Chatterjee	Vice Chairman
Shri Sanjeev Sarna	General Secretary
Shri Vijay Kumar	Treasurer
Shri Vijay Gupta	Joint Secretary
Shri Sandeep Tandon	Joint Secretary
Smt. Urvashi Puri	Joint Secretary
Col. BS Rana	Chief Administrator

APPENDIX III

Manifestations of Haidakhan Babaji

2nd century BCE – Lakulish (said to be the twenty-eight birth of Lord Shiva) appears in Kayavarohan, Gujarat

15th century BCE – Lama Baba appears in Tibet

1840 – Mahavatar Babaji manifests in Kumaon

1861 – Lahiri Mahashaya initiated by Mahavatar Babaji (as described in the 1946 *Autobiography of a Yogi)*

1908 – Mahendra Maharaj is born

1922 – Mahavatar Babaji dematerializes

1969 – Mahendra Maharaj leaves his body

February 1970 – Babaji manifests in Kumaon

14 February 1984 – Babaji leaves his body

APPENDIX IV

Line Map Route to Haidakhan and Ranikhet

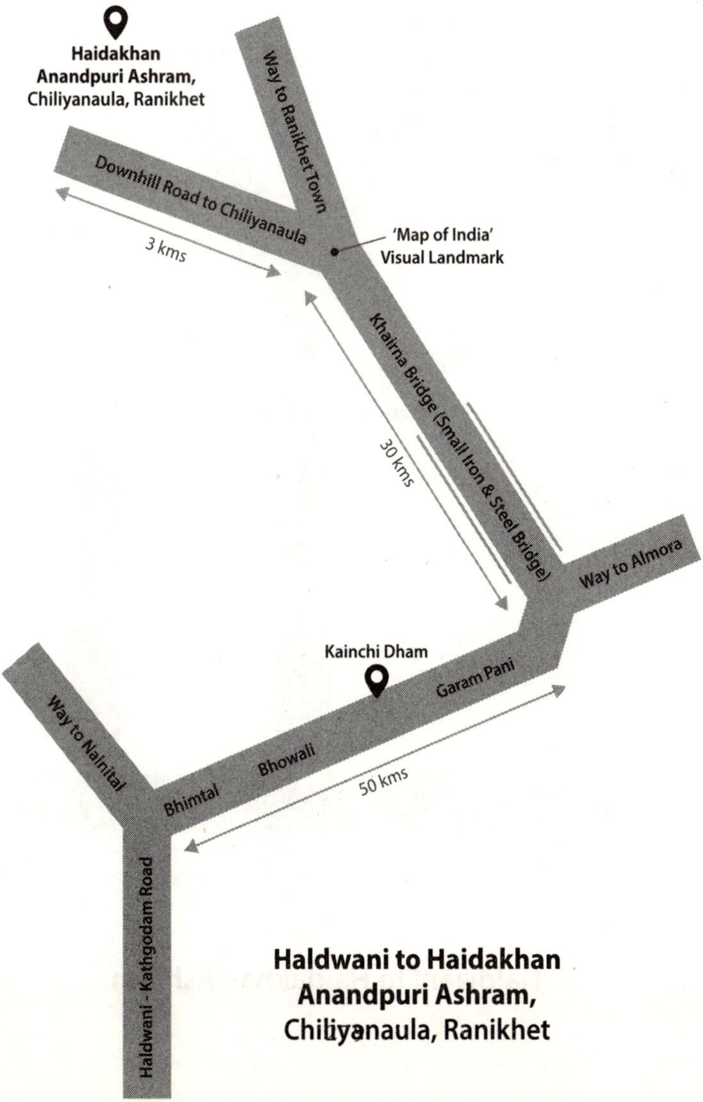

Haldwani to Haidakhan
Anandpuri Ashram,
Chiliyanaula, Ranikhet

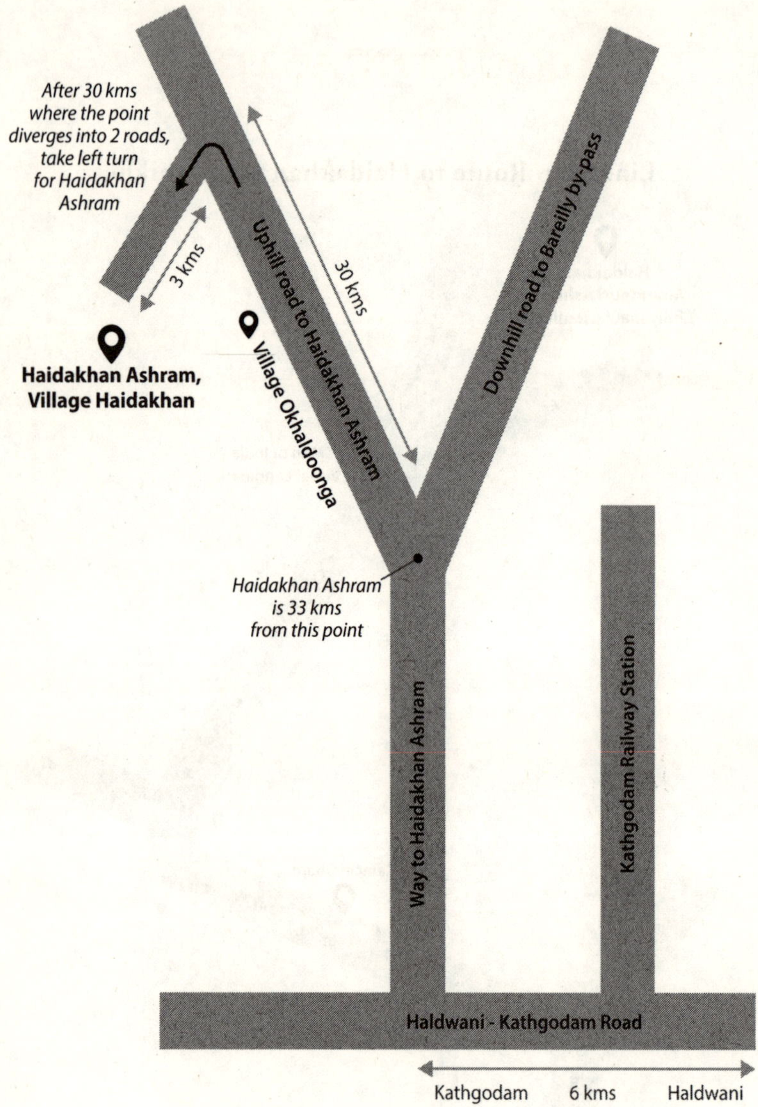

Haldwani to Haidakhan Ashram

ABOUT THE AUTHOR

Vijay Gupta is former Officer on Special Duty (OSD) to the late Congress politician Rajesh Pilot. He is a member of the Haidakhandi Samaj and a direct disciple of Haidakhan Baba. He is a lawyer by profession.

ABOUT THE TRANSLATOR

Namita Kala is a freelance editor and former reporter. She has worked with *The Indian Express* and *The Pioneer* and has written extensively on politics and the environment. She divides her time between Delhi and Dehradun.